DOUGLAS G. SMITH

The Rising Behemoth

Multidistrict and Mass Tort Litigation in the United States

ABA
AMERICAN BAR ASSOCIATION
ABA Publishing

Printed in the United States of America.

24 23 22 21 20   5 4 3 2 1

Library of Congress Cataloging-in-Publication Data

Names: Smith, Douglas G. LLM., author.
Title: The rising behemoth: multidistrict and mass tort litigation in the United States / Douglas G. Smith.
Description: Chicago, Illinois : ABA Publishing, American Bar Association, [2020] | Includes index. | Summary: "Over the last few decades, multidistrict litigation in the federal courts has exploded. Originally a mechanism for consolidating relatively small numbers of commercial cases, with the advent of large-scale mass tort litigation, it has become the primary vehicle for resolving hundreds of thousands of tort claims pending in the federal court system. From asbestos to opioids, MDL proceedings are now used to resolve many of the largest and most high-profile disputes. In recent years, however, participants in multidistrict litigation have expressed significant dissatisfaction. Defendants maintain that MDL proceedings attract large numbers of meritless claims and that many MDL courts are failing to provide sufficient scrutiny to the claims that are filed. As a result, defendants are overwhelmed with large numbers of meritless cases and face significant pressure to settle, providing compensation for many claims that should not have been filed in the first place. From filing to resolution through litigation or settlement, The Rising Behemoth addresses each of the steps in large-scale MDL litigation in the federal courts. In the process, it significantly advances the debate regarding modern MDL practice and offers concrete suggestions for ways in which the system can be improved"– Provided by publisher.
Identifiers: LCCN 2020034509 (print) | LCCN 2020034510 (ebook) | ISBN 9781641057844 (hardcover) | ISBN 9781641057851 (ebook)
Subjects: LCSH: Torts–United States . | Complex litigation–United States. | Class actions (Civil procedure)–United States. | Actions and defenses–United States.
Classification: LCC KF8896 .S65 2020 (print) | LCC KF8896 (ebook) | DDC 346.7303–dc23
LC record available at https://lccn.loc.gov/2020034509
LC ebook record available at https://lccn.loc.gov/2020034510

Discounts are available for books ordered in bulk. Special consideration is given to state bars, CLE programs, and other bar-related organizations. Inquire at Book Publishing, ABA Publishing, American Bar Association, 321 N. Clark Street, Chicago, Illinois 60654-7598.

www.shopABA.org

Praise for THE RISING BEHEMOTH

A rare and much needed comprehensive review of a systemic problem that has plagued the federal courts for over 25 years.

—David Bernick, Partner, Paul, Weiss, Rifkind, Wharton & Garrison LLP

In *The Rising Behemoth*, Douglas G. Smith delivers a thorough analysis of the expansion of multi-district litigation, its risks and limitations, and the alternatives for resolving complex cases. Smith explains how several influential proceedings altered the way that judges and lawyers structure the process today and the potential avenues for improving MDL administration. This book should be valuable to anyone who wants to learn more about the MDL process today.

—S. Todd Brown, Professor of Law and Vice Dean for Academic Affairs, University at Buffalo School of Law

This accessible yet thorough book hits the important issues facing multidistrict litigation today. It can serve as an introduction to those new to MDLs or as a guide to those with more experience. It will be recommended reading for lawyers, judges, policymakers, and academics alike.

—Brian Fitzpatrick, Professor of Law, Vanderbilt Law School

Multidistrict litigation of product liability cases dominates the federal courts, yet it is not well-understood. Doug Smith's book will go a long way toward fixing that problem. Smith explains clearly and concisely how MDL litigation works. Equally important, Smith identifies the grave problems plaguing multidistrict litigation—including indiscriminate filing of baseless cases, unrepresentative "bellwether" trials, and lack of appellate review. As Smith appreciates, these are knotty problems. But they are not insurmountable. Meaningful solutions are desperately needed if MDL litigation is to live up to its laudable purpose—achieving efficiency while preserving the rights of all litigants.

—Max Heerman, Senior Counsel, Litigation, Medtronic

What happens when plaintiffs file thousands of lawsuits alleging harm from a drug or medical device? Douglas Smith provides an illuminating perspective on how courts handle multidistrict and mass tort litigation and the problems that prevent cases from being resolved fairly and efficiently. Smith writes from a defense perspective, but his analysis will be of interest to anyone thinking about the high stakes and sometimes freewheeling world of mass torts. A timely and enormously helpful volume.

—David Noll, Professor of Law, Rutgers Law School

For Renee, Evan, Liam, and Brendan

Contents

Acknowledgments

I would like to thank all of the lawyers from whom I have learned much during my career, including all of the lawyers with whom and against whom I have worked in multidistrict proceedings. In addition, I would like to specifically thank David Bernick, S. Todd Brown, Brian Fitzpatrick, Max Heerman, Mark Herrmann, David Noll, Renee Smith, Karl Stampfl, and Andrew Trask for providing valuable input. In addition, I would like to thank Kathleen Cawley and her team, Jennifer Ahmed, Maria Salinas, Dan McNamara, and Susan Woods, for their technical assistance.

Introduction

Multidistrict litigation (MDL) is exploding in the federal courts. Under this procedural device, thousands of cases sharing common issues may be consolidated for pre-trial proceedings before a single judge. Each year, the federal courts preside over multiple MDL proceedings involving hundreds of thousands of individual cases addressing diverse subject matter. Despite this proliferation of MDL cases, multidistrict litigation is a phenomenon of which few in the general public have ever heard. While many may have seen late-night advertisements on television asking them if they have been injured by asbestos, pharmaceuticals, or other household products, most have not actually been plaintiffs themselves in such cases and, even if they have, most will never set foot in a court presiding over an MDL proceeding.

The MDL procedure started out as an attempt to increase efficiency of large-scale civil litigation by consolidating individual lawsuits that share common issues for pre-trial proceedings before a single judge. The theory was that a single judge would be able to avoid duplicative discovery and would be able to issue consistent rulings that applied to all cases, thus avoiding parallel proceedings occurring in courts throughout the country.

The goals of those responsible for developing this procedure were admirable. However, in recent years, participants in multidistrict litigation have expressed a variety of criticisms. Increasingly, multidistrict litigation is swallowing civil litigation in the federal courts. Data indicate that approximately 50 percent of all civil cases filed in the federal courts are consolidated in multidistrict proceedings.[1] With this consolidation has come the potential for increasing numbers of meritless claims. As numerous participants in the process have observed, aggregation of claims results in less scrutiny provided to each individual claim, which, in turn, can provide an incentive for lawyers to file claims of dubious merit. Because of the reduced scrutiny, claims that normally would not be filed as individual cases may escape rigorous review if they are aggregated with meritorious claims before a single judge. Thus, for example, it is not uncommon for plaintiff counsel to file cases where the plaintiff was never exposed to the product that allegedly caused the injury, where the plaintiff never suffered the alleged injury, or where the statute of limitations that sets the deadline for filing the claim has expired.

In addition, aggregation in MDL proceedings increases the pressure on defendants to settle their claims, and frequently judges presiding over MDL cases view their task as facilitating settlement rather than digging in and addressing the merits of the thousands of claims before them. The sheer volume of claims at issue in an MDL proceeding increases the pressure on defendants to settle. Moreover, because these claims frequently are not subject to the scrutiny given to individual civil cases, there may be little opportunity to narrow the litigation. Critics have charged that the failure to provide such scrutiny and actually adjudicate claims in many MDL proceedings may have adverse consequences for both plaintiffs and defendants alike.

This book discusses the rise of multidistrict litigation and the procedures courts have employed in such proceedings to facilitate their resolution. Many of the largest MDL cases involve mass tort claims—for example, claims alleging that a defendant's products have caused personal injuries to the plaintiffs who filed the claims. However, MDL procedures can apply to any category of cases, as long as the cases share common issues and consolidation for pre-trial proceedings would increase the efficient resolution of those claims. Accordingly, MDLs may involve a variety of subject matters, including antitrust, securities, and consumer fraud.

Chapter 1 discusses the origins of multidistrict litigation and the process by which an MDL proceeding is established. Federal law establishes a Panel comprised of federal judges who decide whether a particular group of cases should be consolidated in a single proceeding. The arguments in front of this Panel largely relate to *which* federal court (and ultimately which judge) should preside over the litigation. However, as the MDL process has come into disfavor among defendants, increasingly, the Panel is hearing objections to creating an MDL proceeding in the first place. Defendants sometimes seek to avoid multidistrict litigation, viewing the process as broken and potentially resulting in coercive settlements and unjust outcomes. While multidistrict litigation was originally designed with antitrust and other types of large commercial cases in mind, with parties increasingly utilizing MDL procedures to resolve personal injury litigation, it has quickly expanded to encompass nearly half of the civil cases filed in the federal court system.

Chapter 2 addresses the increasing concerns over the ability of MDL courts to give sufficient scrutiny to the claims being filed in these proceedings. The rise in multidistrict litigation has been accompanied by an increase in the number of meritless claims filed in these proceedings. A large mass tort litigation may involve thousands of individual claims, a significant percentage of which may not warrant compensation. As commentators have observed, aggregation in general can increase the number of meritless claims filed for a variety of reasons. It can increase such claims by decreasing the scrutiny given to individual cases in an aggregated proceeding. It can also increase such claims by intensifying the pressure on defendants to settle due to the sheer number of cases, which further reduces the scrutiny that otherwise would be applied to individual claims. Critics of the MDL system question whether MDL courts are adequately addressing the problem, as the stakes for litigants caught up in MDL cases continue to grow.

Chapter 3 examines the role of the MDL court in establishing a framework for resolving the claims before it. This process includes establishing a schedule and case-management procedures for the orderly resolution of the proceeding, overseeing the exchange of information by the parties in discovery, and putting in place procedures for the resolution of the claims. Each MDL proceeding presents its own unique circumstances impacting decisions regarding scheduling, case management, discovery, and dispute resolution.

Chapter 4 addresses discovery and exchange of information in an MDL proceeding. As in any other litigation, one of the core aspects of the dispute resolution process is the parties' exchange of information relevant to assessing the validity and value of the claims. In an MDL proceeding, while the dynamics may be different given the sheer number of cases involved, the basic rules are the same. The normal rules of civil procedure that provide for production of documents and testimony are the same in an MDL proceeding as in an individual civil case. However, MDL courts also have developed streamlined procedures to attempt to provide basic information more quickly and efficiently. While these procedures represent valuable supplements to the normal rules of civil procedure, they should not supplant these established rules. Once all parties have access to relevant information about the claims, the MDL court and the parties can then utilize a variety of procedural mechanisms to determine which claims are viable and should proceed.

Chapter 5 begins a discussion of the ways in which MDL courts have assessed the merits of the claims before them. Increasingly, courts presiding over MDL proceedings have come to recognize that such proceedings attract large numbers of meritless claims. As a result, there is now arguably an approaching consensus that MDL courts must employ procedures at the beginning of an MDL proceeding to weed out such claims. One way in which courts have done this is to grant generic motions that address the validity of all, or a subset, of the claims filed in an MDL proceeding. Indeed, one of the primary purposes of the MDL procedure appears to have been to allow courts to resolve such common issues during pre-trial proceedings. Moreover, courts are increasingly receptive to granting such omnibus motions.

Chapter 6 describes procedures MDL courts have employed to address claims on an individual basis. Issues raised in an MDL proceeding are not always common among a large group of claims. Rather, there also are case-specific issues that arise with respect to individual claims. This may involve, for example, whether a particular plaintiff was actually exposed to a particular product or whether a particular plaintiff's specific injury was actually caused by the product. The procedures courts have employed to deal with these case-specific issues are more diverse in nature. In addition to motion practice, courts have used other procedural devices to weed out claims that lack merit or to encourage plaintiffs to dismiss them voluntarily. Such procedures often are employed in parallel with procedures designed to resolve common issues and provide another effective tool for narrowing the scope of the litigation.

Chapter 7 provides an overview of the process employed in many MDL proceedings for taking test cases to trial. Courts in large MDL proceedings frequently attempt to provide the parties with guidance regarding the potential value of the claims in the proceeding by selecting representative "bellwether" cases for trial. The hope is that such trials may help facilitate settlement, and if not, that they will provide the parties the opportunity to prepare materials that can be used in subsequent trials. While many MDL courts have employed such procedures, commentators and participants in MDL proceedings increasingly question their utility, with some going so far as to argue that trying cases within an MDL is contrary to the statutory mandate, which authorizes consolidation solely for pre-trial proceedings. In the future, this debate may result in a decline in the use of such bellwether trials as a means of resolving claims in MDL proceedings.

Chapter 8 discusses settlement in the context of MDL proceedings. The accepted wisdom is that most claims in MDL proceedings are resolved through settlement. However, as noted, courts are increasingly interested in weeding out meritless claims before any settlement is reached. Moreover, the settlement of claims in MDL proceedings has been criticized for a variety of reasons. Defendants note the inordinate pressure an MDL places on them to settle claims that lack merit, while plaintiff advocates suggest the settlement process favors lead plaintiff counsel at the expense of the plaintiffs themselves and lacks important procedural protections to ensure settlements are fair and equitable.

Chapter 9 explains some of the reasons MDL proceedings have encountered difficulty in moving toward resolution. One of the factors that is important for the successful resolution of an MDL proceeding is a significant level of engagement and activity by the presiding judge, who must not only administer but resolve potentially thousands of cases involving complicated and substantial issues. Where judges fail to engage, perhaps in the hope that the parties will eventually settle, MDLs tend to linger without resolution. Another phenomenon that has led to problems with multidistrict litigation is the lack of complete centralization. The MDL procedure only applies to courts in the federal system. In many cases involving federal multidistrict litigation, there may be significant parallel state court proceedings. In such circumstances, state court litigation may interfere with progress in the MDL proceeding. Finally, even after MDL proceedings are settled, there may be problems with settlement administration. Not surprisingly, there have been prominent examples in which meritless, or even fraudulent, claims have received considerable compensation.

Chapter 10 addresses the more substantial criticisms of the MDL process and proposals for reform seeking to address them. While defendants originally viewed MDL proceedings as a potentially more efficient means of addressing large numbers of claims and avoiding duplicative proceedings, they increasingly see MDLs as oriented toward settlement and as failing to provide the necessary scrutiny to claims. Citing statistics showing that 30 to 40 percent of cases are not meeting basic requirements for stating a claim, defendants have proposed a series of reforms such as requiring plaintiffs to make a basic showing early in the litigation demonstrating that they can prove fundamental elements of their claims, mandating review of key MDL court rulings by an appeals court during the course of the MDL, and requiring the parties' consent before cases are tried in an MDL proceeding. While these formal proposals have not yet been implemented, the future may see significant changes in MDL procedures. At a minimum, the debate over reforming the system is likely to continue and to encourage judges presiding over MDL proceedings to implement procedures on their own that will address some of these criticisms within the existing legal framework.

Chapter 11 discusses some of the potential alternatives to multidistrict litigation. One obvious alternative is to litigate claims on an individual basis. However, unless the MDL procedure is abolished, this alternative is not likely to be employed and it may result in significant inefficiencies. A second alternative is the class action procedure. However, existing constraints make class actions an unlikely alternative, given that the diversity of claims in most MDL proceedings makes certification of a class to resolve the litigation less than feasible. Finally, the bankruptcy system provides a potential alternative for companies overwhelmed with large numbers of claims. However, while bankruptcy provides many advantages, there are downsides for corporate defendants selecting this option, and it frequently is not the first alternative for companies facing significant liability.

In sum, multidistrict litigation arguably has reached a point of inflection. Increasingly, massive proceedings such as those addressing claims involving opioid addiction or allegations that popular weed killers cause lymphoma have attracted the public's attention. The corporate community sees a litigation landscape it believes leads to results that are inconsistent with the merits of the claims and which, in some cases, are arbitrary. Plaintiffs' law firms are provided with an increasingly greater incentive to bring ever-larger numbers of claims, while simultaneously conceding that in many cases there are problems with the filing of claims that lack merit. A handful of repeat players have amassed significant wealth as the result of a system that is arguably in need of improvement. This book attempts to shed light on the ongoing debate.

1
The Rise of Multidistrict Litigation

The MDL procedure is a mechanism for centralizing federal cases involving common issues that has been around for decades. Established by federal statute in 1968, the impetus behind the procedure was to achieve efficiency by avoiding duplicative proceedings involving similar cases spread throughout the federal court system.[2] As the Supreme Court has recognized, the statute sought to "eliminate duplication in discovery, avoid conflicting rulings and schedules, reduce litigation cost, and save the time and effort of the parties, the attorneys, the witnesses, and the courts."[3] It thus represented a significant innovation in federal civil procedure that the drafters hoped would achieve significant cost savings and avoid inconsistency.

Prior to the statute, individual cases that were related in some way might be filed in different federal courts across the country, proceeding in parallel. Courts could attempt to informally coordinate with one another, but this did not always happen and, even if it did, there would still be inefficiencies. As a result, there was a potential for duplicative proceedings where the same witnesses gave testimony over and over again and the parties produced the same or similar documents multiple times. There also was the potential that different courts might issue inconsistent rulings on the same issues in related proceedings. Even though decisions issued in another jurisdiction might have a persuasive effect on courts addressing similar issues, they would not necessarily be binding in other proceedings. This inefficiency and potential for inconsistency could be eliminated if related cases were sent to a single judge who could then coordinate pre-trial proceedings and avoid duplicative efforts.

While cases within a given federal district could be sent to a single judge within that district, there was no effective mechanism for sending cases in multiple jurisdictions to a single judge in a single district. Accordingly, the MDL statute filled a gap in federal practice that arguably had led to significant inefficiency in the federal court system. As the years progressed, the need for such a procedural mechanism grew as the scope of litigation involving related cases increased. MDL courts moved from presiding over relatively small numbers of coordinated antitrust and other commercial cases to mass tort litigation involving potentially thousands of individual personal injury cases.

Rise of the MDL Procedure

Today, MDL proceedings are a prominent feature of civil practice in the federal court system. Indeed, for some sorts of litigation such as pharmaceutical and medical device litigation, MDL proceedings are the primary forum in which such cases are litigated. While there may be parallel state court litigation, the MDL is often the central forum in which such litigation is resolved. As several commentators have observed, the "MDL has replaced the class action as the foremost mechanism for resolving mass-tort disputes in the federal courts."[4]

Indeed, the MDL procedure has had a sweeping impact on civil litigation in the federal courts. Data analyzed by Duke Law School's Bolch Judicial Institute show that nearly half of all civil cases pending in the federal system now are collected in MDL proceedings. Moreover, the rate of growth of MDLs in recent years has been significant: "More than 40% of the civil cases pending in the nation's federal courts are consolidated in multidistrict litigations. In 2017, these MDL cases ma[d]e up 42% of the pending civil caseload. In 2002, that number was 16%."[5]

As the scope of multidistrict litigation continues to grow, the importance of the procedures employed in MDL proceedings continues to increase, as does the scrutiny applied to such proceedings.

The amount written about MDL proceedings continues to increase along with the interest in such proceedings. Likewise, there is renewed interest in efforts to improve or reform MDL procedures.

Nonetheless, the MDL statute does not accomplish a complete centralization of litigation in every case. The statute provides only for centralization of cases pending in federal court. Frequently, in the sort of large-scale litigation that is the subject of modern MDL proceedings, there will be parallel proceedings filed in state court asserting similar claims. While parties may seek to remove cases originally filed in state court to federal court and then transfer them to the MDL proceeding, there must be a federal jurisdictional basis for such removals, and accordingly such attempts are not always successful. There may be an ongoing battle among the parties during the course of an MDL proceeding over whether individual cases that continue to be filed in state court should be removed to federal court and transferred to the MDL proceeding. Because efforts to remove those cases may not always be successful, it is frequently the case that there are ongoing state court proceedings in parallel with federal MDLs.

In fact, some lawyers representing plaintiffs in large mass tort litigation prefer to pursue their cases in state court and aggressively seek to keep cases in state court in the face of defense efforts to remove them. While sometimes these will be individual cases filed in different state court jurisdictions, there may also be parallel consolidated proceedings that involve multiple cases pending before a single state court judge, much like an MDL proceeding in federal court. Indeed, many states have adopted procedures similar to federal MDL procedures, and it is increasingly common to have consolidated state court proceedings in parallel with a consolidated federal MDL. Such consolidated state court proceedings may change the dynamics of an MDL proceeding significantly. Thus, while the MDL procedure goes a long way to centralize litigation, it frequently does not achieve complete centralization.

The centralization that is achieved through the MDL procedure is also limited temporally. The statute contemplates that cases will be returned to the courts from which they were transferred once the MDL court has completed its work. Moreover, as commentators have observed, the statute specifically authorizes consolidation for "pretrial" purposes, implying that the statute as originally conceived did not contemplate that the MDL court would be presiding over trials as part of an MDL.[6] Thus, while there is a history of courts conducting trials as part of MDL proceedings, some commentators have gone so far as to argue that this activity exceeds the scope of the courts' authority.[7] Rather, they argue that MDL courts are limited to deciding pre-trial issues and do not have jurisdiction to take a case through trial unless it was originally filed in the MDL court itself.

Establishing the MDL Proceeding

The criteria for establishing an MDL proceeding are fairly straightforward. Under the federal statute establishing MDL proceedings, a group of cases must share one or more common questions of law or fact and transfer must further the "just and efficient conduct of such actions."[8] The plain language of the statute illustrates that the MDL framework was oriented toward resolution of common issues. It was not simply designed as a mechanism for getting all claims together in one location and forcing a settlement. Rather, the drafters contemplated that the MDL court would preside over a range of issues that normally arise during the course of civil cases during the pre-trial phase. This would include discovery as well as dispositive motion practice. Accordingly, the range of matters that may be taken up in an MDL proceeding is significant.

Whether an MDL will be created is decided by the Judicial Panel on Multidistrict Litigation (JPML), a group of sitting federal court judges who meet several times a year to consider requests for MDL consolidation. Either plaintiffs or defendants may file a transfer motion with the Panel to create an MDL proceeding. The Panel then receives briefing and hears arguments from all interested parties regarding whether the statutory criteria are met for creating an MDL proceeding, and if so, the proper location for such a proceeding.

While historically obtaining MDL treatment for a group of related claims was not particularly difficult, in recent years defendants increasingly have fought MDL consolidation. In the past, defendants would frequently be the ones who sought an MDL proceeding to provide more organization and structure to the litigation and to avoid the potential for duplicative proceedings in multiple jurisdictions. The efficiency of the MDL process benefited defendants by reducing the costs associated with litigation, both financial and in terms of the time a defendant devoted to the litigation.

However, over time, the views of the defense bar shifted. Defendants increasingly viewed MDL proceedings as degenerating into mechanisms for forcing settlement without subjecting filed claims to the normal scrutiny that accompanies litigation of individual cases in the federal court system. The perceived costs of MDL treatment began to outweigh the potential benefits. As a result, fights over the creation of MDL proceedings now are more common. In some instances, the Panel will hear repeated requests for the creation of an MDL proceeding as additional cases are filed.[9] While the Panel may decide that creation of an MDL proceeding is inappropriate in the early stages of a litigation, as cases accumulate, the Panel may become convinced there are sufficient numbers to warrant an MDL proceeding. In other cases, the litigation may remain more constrained, and an MDL proceeding may never be initiated.

Thus, for example, the Panel may decide that an MDL proceeding is not warranted where there are very few cases filed and there is presently no indication the litigation will achieve a sufficient magnitude to warrant an MDL proceeding. While centralization increases efficiency, it also removes cases from the jurisdiction where plaintiffs chose to file them and where venue may be more appropriate. As the Panel has observed, "where . . . there are a minimal number of cases involved in the litigation the moving party bears a strong burden to show that the common questions of fact are so complex and the accompanying common discovery so time-consuming as to overcome the inconvenience to the party whose action is being transferred and its witnesses."[10] Accordingly, unless a sufficient number of cases are filed, the Panel may reject MDL consolidation. In such circumstances, the federal courts that have the individual cases can still engage in informal coordination to achieve some of the same efficiencies that would be achieved from sending the cases to a single judge presiding over an MDL proceeding.

Likewise, the Panel may reject a request for MDL consolidation where the cases do not have a sufficient nexus of common issues. Where the cases involve relatively diverse sets of facts and common issues do not predominate, they may not be appropriate for MDL consolidation, particularly where there are not a large number of cases. As the Panel has explained, in cases where "it appears that individualized facts . . . will predominate over the common factual issues alleged by plaintiffs," consolidation of cases in an MDL proceeding may not be appropriate.[11]

In most litigations, however, the primary fight among the parties is over the location of the MDL proceeding. Under the statute, the Panel is charged with selecting the judicial district in which an MDL will be created.[12] However, the Panel typically sends the cases to a particular judge within the district. The choice of the judge that will preside over an MDL proceeding can have significant consequences. When cases are spread among multiple judges throughout the federal court system, there will be the potential for a greater range of outcomes. When cases are sent to a single judge, that judge exercises a great deal of influence. The judge's decisions on pre-trial motions can have significant effects on the litigation. Likewise, the judge's decision with respect to the scope and timing of discovery can impact the cost as well as the outcome of the litigation.

Accordingly, the parties frequently put forth a significant effort in researching the potential judges who may be candidates for the MDL proceeding, as well as advocating in favor of their preferred judge. This sometimes leads to multiple judges being proposed by various parties in the litigation. Plaintiff counsel may not be uniform in terms of their choice of judge, and indeed may have significant incentives to disagree on the proposed forum for the MDL. Plaintiff counsel may seek to have the MDL established where they have pending cases so they can increase their role in the MDL proceeding and potentially be selected by the MDL court as lead counsel. Moreover, there may be genuine disagreements among counsel regarding whether a particular judge is better for their clients than proposed alternatives.

As we will see, some of the current criticisms of multidistrict litigation focus on this aspect of the MDL proceeding. The fact that multiple cases go to a single decision maker makes the stakes particularly significant for both plaintiffs and defendants. That single decision maker can completely terminate the litigation at the pre-trial stage, nullifying the investment plaintiff counsel have made in the cases. This can have significant financial consequences for the lawyers involved, who frequently are working on contingency fees and may advance the costs of pursuing the litigation in anticipation of a share of the proceeds when the litigation concludes. Conversely, the judge presiding over the MDL proceeding may issue rulings that can greatly disadvantage the defendants. The court may deny pre-trial motions seeking to dismiss the claims, or at least narrow the scope of the litigation. It may also issue discovery orders that can adversely impact defendants. In the most extreme cases, MDL courts have sanctioned defendants for failing to preserve or produce documents, which, in turn, has had significant adverse consequences for defendants in the litigation.[13] Accordingly, all sides recognize that the nature of the decision maker can have a significant impact on the course of an MDL proceeding.

Consequently, the Panel's decision regarding where to establish the MDL is one that is significant and, unfortunately, is a decision that may be subject to a certain degree of arbitrariness. In making this decision, the Panel considers a number of factors, including where the current cases are pending, the workload of the judges who have those cases, the judges' experience with MDL proceedings, the convenience of the parties and the parties' preferences regarding each forum, where documents and witnesses are likely to be located, and how far along each of the pending cases is in terms of resolution.[14]

Under this framework, plaintiffs have some degree of control over where the MDL is established. One tactic plaintiffs may pursue is to file a cluster of cases in a particular jurisdiction where they would like to see the MDL sent so that the jurisdiction has the most pending cases and cases that are further along than cases filed in other jurisdictions. This type of forum shopping may influence the selection of the forum for the MDL proceeding, given that these are factors the Panel considers in deciding whether to establish the MDL proceeding. In contrast, defendants most likely have less ability to influence the facts the Panel may take into consideration in deciding where to set up the MDL proceeding. Defendants may be limited to advocating in favor of their preferred forum based on the facts they are given.

Likewise, while the selection process is sometimes less than transparent, it appears that lobbying from various members of the judiciary also can contribute to the location of an MDL proceeding. Appointment to an MDL proceeding can be a prestigious and interesting assignment for a district judge. Accordingly, it has been suggested by some that certain members of the judiciary may actively seek out such appointments and may in effect lobby the Panel to receive them.[15] Conversely, there may be other members of the judiciary who would be very good candidates for an MDL proceeding who may not have an interest in receiving an appointment and who may therefore resist efforts to appoint them. Accordingly, there is the potential that the selection of the MDL forum may depend, at least in part, on factors not contemplated by those establishing the system.

Once an MDL is established, pending cases are transferred to the district where the MDL has been set up. However, new plaintiffs typically will continue to file individual cases that relate to an MDL proceeding even after it is formed. As mentioned, these cases may be filed in state court and then removed to federal court, or they may be filed directly in federal courts other than the MDL court presiding over the litigation. The drafters of the MDL statute contemplated this eventuality and provided that subsequently filed cases could be transferred to the MDL court. Accordingly, transfer orders may be issued as cases are filed. The parties, however, have an opportunity to object before the Panel to avoid transfer if they can show their case is not related to the MDL proceeding and therefore should not be transferred. Typically, though, it is fairly clear which cases belong in the MDL proceeding, and the process of transferring subsequently filed cases becomes largely an administrative matter. Cases continue to populate the MDL docket as new cases are filed and transferred to the MDL court, and cases may also be filed directly with the MDL court itself.

However, there is at least one potential wrinkle that can sometimes occur in this process. Requests for transfer to an MDL proceeding are not immediately granted. As cases are filed, there is a lag between the time the Panel receives notice of the cases and when they are transferred. This lag allows the parties time to file any objections to transfer and affords the Panel time to rule on any objections filed. In situations in which the cases subject to transfer were originally filed in state court and then removed to federal court, there is frequently a race between defendants who seek to transfer the cases to an MDL proceeding and plaintiffs who seek remand back to state court as soon as possible. As soon as a case is removed, plaintiffs may file a motion to remand in the federal court that has the pending case.

The federal court that has the case has a choice to make at that point. Either it will hear the remand motion immediately and potentially send the case back to state court before it can be transferred to the MDL court, or it can stay the proceedings pending transfer or simply not rule on the motion, in which case the remand motion will be resolved by the MDL court. Accordingly, while federal courts in this situation frequently end up deferring any ruling to allow the MDL court to decide the issue, the current system injects some level of uncertainty and perhaps unnecessary litigation over whether to stay pending remand motions. In most cases, however, transfer to the MDL court is merely an administrative matter, and in large litigations, the MDL court can expect that there will be a steady stream of transferred cases as new cases are filed.

2
The Rise of Meritless Claims

One of the most fundamental challenges facing multidistrict litigation is the proliferation of claims that lack merit. One of the potential downsides of an MDL proceeding is that, as with any litigation, centralization or aggregation of cases can provide an incentive for increased filing and a reduction in the amount of review given to each individual case. As review of each case is reduced, there is a greater incentive to file claims that are of questionable merit in the hope they will escape review. Those MDL courts that are not active in screening cases therefore encourage the accumulation of large numbers of claims that may not be valid. This phenomenon has led some critics of MDL procedures to conclude that, "[i]nstead of improving judicial efficiency and achieving just resolution of litigation as Congress intended, the MDL device has developed into a black hole that attracts and warehouses claims."[16]

Factors Leading to the Increase in Meritless Claims

There are many reasons the number of meritless claims filed in MDL proceedings has increased. Most fundamentally, lawyers have a financial incentive to file as many claims as possible in an MDL proceeding. The more claims filed, the more money ultimately may flow into the lawyers' pockets, given that their payment is typically based on a contingency fee that awards them a percentage of each plaintiff's recovery. Moreover, as we will see, there is little incentive not to file unsubstantiated claims because lawyers are not punished for doing so or given any financial disincentive that would discourage such filings. Quite the contrary, in many MDL proceedings meritless claims are escaping review and ultimately participating in global settlements that provide them significant compensation.

This financial incentive is magnified by the procedures typically employed in an MDL proceeding.[17] Not only do some courts fail to provide sufficient scrutiny to the filed cases, but they implement procedures that may reward plaintiff law firms for maximizing the number of claims they file in the MDL. As discussed below, MDL courts typically appoint committees comprised of lead plaintiff counsel who do much of the work in the MDL proceeding. These lawyers, in turn, typically receive additional compensation in the form of a percentage of the payments received by all plaintiffs in the litigation.

One of the factors courts generally look at in appointing lead counsel is the number of cases they have filed. Courts seek to ensure the lawyers serving in these leadership positions have a sufficient incentive to pursue the litigation vigorously. Accordingly, additional compensation frequently turns on the number of cases a law firm files in the MDL. In addition, a position on these committees also gives a law firm a role in controlling the litigation and may lead to lucrative leadership positions in future MDLs, as lead lawyers tend to be picked from the same stable of repeat players. Law firms that are not members of these leadership committees generally have little say over the direction of the litigation and do not share in the significant financial rewards that flow to members of these leadership committees.

Aside from the financial incentives to file ever-increasing numbers of cases, another reason claims continue to increase is the track record of failure by some MDL courts to adequately screen the cases filed in large MDL proceedings. The more cases at issue in an MDL proceeding, the more difficult it is for the law firms that file them to adequately screen them before filing. The emergence of mega-MDLs, typically involving mass tort claims alleging personal injuries, has led to increased demands on the limited resources available to plaintiff law firms to screen the cases they file. The result has been an increase in the number of cases filed in MDL proceedings that were not adequately screened by the law firms that filed them.

Other factors, such as the proliferation of advertising and the availability of third-party litigation financing, exacerbate the situation and further facilitate the filing of increasingly large numbers of cases. Plaintiff law firms today are essentially able to purchase cases from companies that conduct mass advertising. Law firms are not simply sitting back and waiting for clients to contact them; rather, they are reaching out to generate claims among a population that may not have thought to file a lawsuit absent advertising encouraging them to do so.

In addition, with the proliferation of third-party funders, law firms are able to purchase these cases using other people's money. Litigation funders will finance the purchase of the cases in exchange for a share of the ultimate compensation received. As a result, plaintiff law firms may put up little money themselves. This state of affairs has led critics of the current MDL system to argue that, "we cannot underestimate the role litigation funding is playing in increasing the aggregation of claims. The availability of easy money has allowed certain plaintiffs' attorneys to take huge risks on less meritorious claims without having much, or maybe any, of their own money at stake."[18]

Indeed, most people have seen advertisements on late-night television seeking to recruit individuals to file claims alleging personal injuries caused by various products. Frequently, these advertisements promise recovery of potentially millions of dollars with little or no work on the part of the individual plaintiffs, suggesting that cases likely will be settled without having to go to court. These cases are often sold off in bulk to other law firms that represent the individual plaintiffs. The active recruiting of potential plaintiffs leads to increased filing of cases and increases the time required for review and screening of asserted claims. Absent diligence by the lawyers who ultimately file the cases, it is easy to see how unsubstantiated claims might result from this process.

Certain realities of modern MDL practice may also provide plaintiff counsel with a disincentive to screen cases adequately before filing them or, indeed, to file cases of dubious merit. Plaintiff firms know that because there is only a single decision maker presiding over potentially thousands of claims, the MDL court has a limited ability to screen the cases. Every instance in which an MDL court fails to provide rigorous scrutiny of filed cases only increases the probability that plaintiff firms will receive compensation regardless of the merit of the claims they file. Centralization of cases before a single judge creates a potential bottleneck, preventing scrutiny of the filed claims that may incentivize plaintiffs to file claims regardless of their merit. As some commentators have argued, "MDL consolidation for products liability actions does have the unintended consequence of producing more new case filings of marginal merit in federal court, many of which would not have been filed otherwise."[19]

The fact that many MDLs result in some form of global settlement further incentivizes plaintiffs to file cases regardless of their merit. The fact that settlement rather than litigation and scrutiny of the claims is the ultimate outcome of many MDLs means plaintiffs will be incentivized to file as many cases as possible to maximize their recovery under any subsequent settlement. As we will see, while global settlements in MDL proceedings sometimes impose requirements that claims must meet to receive compensation, the level of scrutiny under any settlement is likely much less than the claims would receive in an adversarial proceeding before the court. Even though there are examples showing that many cases filed in MDLs do not meet even the relatively relaxed criteria for receiving compensation applied by many settlements, nonetheless the chances of recovery are higher than if the cases were litigated in the court system.

Accordingly, the fact that many MDLs result in settlement increases the probability of payment for meritless claims and, in turn, incentivizes plaintiffs to file greater numbers of claims that lack merit. As one judge has recognized, "[s]ome lawyers seem to think that their case will be swept into the MDL where a global settlement will be reached, allowing them to obtain a recovery without the individual merit of their case being scrutinized as closely as it would if it proceeded as a separate individual action."[20] This phenomenon can be exacerbated where the judge presiding over the MDL proceeding fails to take an active role in scrutinizing claims or where the judge indicates that the goal of the proceeding is settlement, rather than litigation of the individual claims.

Increase in the Number of Claims

All of these factors work together to put upward pressure on the number of claims generated by multidistrict litigation and, in fact, the data show that there has been an explosion in the number of cases filed in MDL proceedings. Recent estimates indicate almost half of civil cases filed in federal courts now are part of MDL proceedings.[21] Moreover, the number of cases is up dramatically from just a decade or two ago. Accordingly, both the number of cases and the rate at which they are filed have increased over recent years.

This increase has continued despite the fact that there has been some rotation among the types of claims pending in MDL cases. For example, while thousands of asbestos personal injury claims were shuttled to an MDL that was one of the largest at the time, after the MDL court resolved thousands of those claims, it terminated the MDL. The slack was picked up by thousands of medical device claims alleging that various surgical mesh products caused personal injuries, as medical device MDLs became more common. Most recently, government entities and other plaintiffs have filed large MDLs seeking to recover costs allegedly resulting from the sale of prescription opioids and alleging personal injuries stemming from the weed killer Roundup. Each MDL presents its own unique issues and challenges. Despite this diversity, what is striking is the relatively consistent stream of cases flowing into MDLs in the federal system.

As a result, multidistrict proceedings play an increasingly important role in the resolution of civil litigation in the federal courts. The growing significance of multidistrict litigation has resulted in a corresponding rise in the level of scrutiny given to such proceedings. Practitioners, law professors, and members of the judiciary have begun to speak out and discuss multidistrict litigation and the ways in which it may be improved. Likewise, multidistrict litigation is increasingly a topic of academic and practice-oriented publications. As discussed later in this book, this public debate has resulted in a series of proposals to reform and improve the system. It also has resulted in the development of proposed guidelines and best practices courts may follow utilizing their current authority to formulate procedures in MDL proceedings.

With this growing scrutiny, there has been a corresponding increase in the public criticism of MDL proceedings. Defendants have increasingly criticized certain MDL judges as improperly viewing MDLs as being oriented toward settlement. In their opinion, some judges appointed to lead MDL proceedings view their jobs as attempting to get the parties to settle their cases. Similarly, they note that some judges appear hesitant to remand cases to the transferor courts at the end of an MDL, but rather seek to resolve the litigation through a negotiated settlement.

As a result, many defendants believe the pressure to settle has only increased. This orientation of some in the judiciary, along with the growing number of claims and the potential for jackpot verdicts, all work to intensify the pressure on defendants to settle an MDL proceeding. To the extent the court presiding over an MDL proceeding fails to scrutinize the inventory of claims and eliminate cases that have no merit, that pressure can be overwhelming. Yet, defendants are resistant to settle a large body of claims they believe contains many claims that should not receive compensation.

Moreover, the increase in the number of claims only further facilitates the expansion of the number of meritless claims that flood the system. As the number of cases in MDL proceedings grows, the scrutiny given to each individual case decreases, and the ability of meritless claims to evade review only increases. Accordingly, defendants have described MDLs as lawsuit magnets that encourage the filing of meritless claims by flooding the system with cases and reducing the ability of courts to provide the necessary scrutiny to the asserted claims.[22] Defendants therefore criticize the current system as compelling settlements that result in compensation for an increasingly large number of unsubstantiated claims.

However, some critics of the current system argue that plaintiffs likewise are not well-served by MDL proceedings. Professor Elizabeth Chamblee Burch, for example, argues that plaintiffs frequently get lost in large MDL proceedings among the masses of claims. Plaintiff counsel often fail to give plaintiffs in MDL cases the individualized attention they would otherwise receive in an individual case filed in federal court. More concerning, plaintiffs who have meritorious claims may receive less in the way of compensation when settlements are shared with plaintiffs bringing claims that lack merit. The lawyers have an incentive to maximize recovery because they are working on contingency but do not necessarily have an incentive to ensure that claims deserving compensation are maximized while claims that do not deserve compensation are eliminated. The allocation of compensation among the plaintiff population once a settlement is reached is frequently a less than rigorous process that in some cases may result in unfairness. Accordingly, the failure to weed out meritless claims can also harm plaintiffs who might otherwise receive larger recoveries if such scrutiny were applied to the claims in an MDL proceeding or if they brought their cases individually in another forum. According to Professor Burch, the failure to litigate cases in certain MDL proceedings is one of the fundamental problems afflicting modern MDL practice.[23]

Indeed, some critics of the current system have gone even further, suggesting that the aggregate nature of litigation and settlement in MDL proceedings may even violate due process. Thus, for example, Professor Martin Redish has argued that, "MDL, as currently structured . . . infringes on individual claimants' procedural due process rights."[24] These critics contrast MDL proceedings with class actions under Federal Rule of Civil Procedure 23, in which there are certain formalized procedures that at least attempt to protect the due process rights of absent class members. In the MDL context, they argue, such due process concerns are given much less consideration.

While class actions are not completely analogous to MDL proceedings, critics argue that some of the same concerns apply to the two procedural devices. In a class action, the class is represented by certain named plaintiffs and their counsel, and many plaintiffs who are absent are not formally before the court. In an MDL proceeding, in contrast, plaintiffs maintain their individual cases in the MDL and continue to be represented by their own lawyers. However, critics argue that many of these lawyers are sidelined as lead plaintiff counsel make decisions in conjunction with the defendants that may disadvantage, or at least significantly impact, other plaintiffs in the litigation. As greater numbers of claims are filed in an MDL proceeding, these concerns regarding lack of active participation and adequacy of representation only increase. Accordingly, these commentators maintain, the proliferation of cases in MDL proceedings not only raises practical concerns regarding the increase in meritless claims, but also may potentially raise constitutional concerns as well.

Judges who have presided over large MDL proceedings have recognized some of these developing trends and have raised concerns as well. While judges who are assigned to MDLs may not always recognize the potential problems at the outset of an MDL proceeding, frequently toward the end of the process they have a better understanding of the moral hazards inherent in multidistrict litigation. For example, Judge Eduardo Robreno, who presided over one of the largest MDL proceedings involving claims that asbestos products cause disease, concluded, based on his first-hand experience, that there were significant problems regarding meritless claims as well as significant due process concerns: "Aside from the significant due process issues raised by forcing parties to litigate or settle cases in groups, aggregation promotes the filing of cases of uncertain merit. The incentive becomes the number of cases that can be filed, not the relative merit of the individual case."[25] Similarly, Chief Judge Clay Land of the U.S. District Court for the Middle District of Georgia observed in a medical device MDL that, because of the settlement orientation of some MDLs, there has been an incentive to file cases that would not otherwise have been filed if no MDL were created: "This phenomenon produces the perverse result that an MDL, which was established in part to manage cases more efficiently to achieve judicial economy, becomes populated with many non-meritorious cases that must nevertheless be managed by the transferee judge—cases that likely never would have entered the federal court system without the MDL."[26] As Judge Land observed, the increase in meritless claims directly undermines one of the advantages of the MDL proceeding—judicial efficiency.

In fact, the federal judges serving on the Judicial Panel on Multidistrict Litigation themselves have recognized these problems. In defending the current system for resolving MDL proceedings, the Panel has argued that the judges presiding over MDL cases are more than capable of reviewing the claims filed and weeding out claims that lack merit. Thus, the Panel has argued that the process of MDL centralization itself is a superior means of eliminating meritless claims, contending that, "[t]he response to such concerns more properly inheres in assigning all related actions to one judge committed to disposing of spurious claims quickly."[27]

As the Panel has explained, the MDL court is certainly in no worse position to assess the viability of asserted claims than judges presiding over individual cases outside an MDL. MDL judges have equal access to the tools available under the Federal Rules of Civil Procedure and the same inherent judicial powers as other judges and may have superior information by virtue of the fact that they are presiding over multiple cases: "[T]he transferee court handling several cases in an MDL likely is in a better position—and certainly is in no worse position than courts in multiple districts handling individual cases—to properly address meritless claims. There are many tools a transferee court may use to accomplish this task."[28] Accordingly, while establishing an MDL may result in increased claiming, and indeed an increase in meritless claims, in the view of the Panel at least, MDL courts can handle the additional work associated with the creation of an MDL. Moreover, in the Panel's view, this increase in workload does not offset the many benefits associated with an MDL proceeding.

The Consequences of Failing to Address Meritless Claims

As the Panel's comments suggest, elimination of meritless claims early in the MDL proceeding is critical. Not only is the existence of numerous meritless claims in an MDL proceeding a problem in its own right, but it can reduce the efficiency of the MDL process. As meritless claims clog the system, there is less ability to give them the proper treatment they deserve. As the number of cases increases, so do the tendency to forego the normal rules of civil procedure and the pressure to reach a negotiated settlement. The process becomes more cumbersome and takes more time. There are a greater number of stakeholders whose voices must be heard in determining how the litigation will play out. Coordination among counsel becomes more difficult, and judges frequently can feel overwhelmed by the daunting process before them.

Thus, to make progress in an MDL proceeding, it is necessary to identify the universe of claims really at issue in the case. Allowing claims to linger in the proceeding, sometimes referred to as warehousing, can interfere with the efficient resolution of an MDL in multiple ways.

First, the failure to weed out claims that do not belong in the MDL is really a breakdown in the normal litigation process. Under the federal rules that govern civil litigation, typically defendants file motions to dismiss that challenge the legal basis for the asserted claims and then, after discovery has been obtained, file motions for summary judgment that challenge the claims' factual basis. Thus, the normal rules of civil procedure contemplate that claims will be scrutinized early in the proceedings, and the failure of some MDL courts to apply such scrutiny represents a breakdown in the system. In sum, an MDL court should be able to accomplish *more* progress in a given case than would be achieved if the case had never been consolidated in an MDL and continued to be litigated on an individual basis. To the extent the MDL court achieves *less* progress during pre-trial proceedings, it represents a failure of the MDL system.

Another obvious negative effect of failing to address and remove meritless claims from the inventory is the payment of significant sums of money for those claims in the event a settlement is reached. Such payments obviously represent an injustice to the defendants who are paying money for cases that should not receive compensation. More fundamentally, they represent an inefficiency that is somewhat unique to aggregated litigation. If the claims had been addressed individually in the federal courts, it is highly likely that such unwarranted sums would not be paid. In addition, such payments may represent an injustice to plaintiffs who have claims that deserve compensation. Depending on how allocation decisions are ultimately made, every dollar paid to an undeserving claimant is potentially a dollar out of the pocket of a deserving claimant. The injustice of this scenario is exacerbated by the fact that attorneys' fees and costs are removed from the payments received by the plaintiffs. Accordingly, it is entirely possible that a claimant with a valid claim may receive no compensation after fees and costs in a world where non-meritorious claims receive compensation, whereas that same plaintiff might actually recover in a world where meritless claims are removed from the inventory. Thus, the inclusion of non-meritorious claims in an MDL inventory ultimately may lead to significantly reduced or no compensation for plaintiffs whose cases have merit.

Even where those responsible for allocating settlement funds attempt to take such dynamics into account, the presence of meritless claims in the inventory certainly causes significant problems that would not otherwise exist if the normal rules were applied. It is difficult to tell claimants they will receive no compensation or they will receive much less compensation than other plaintiffs where there is news of a multimillion-dollar settlement—even where the claimant has a claim that lacks merit. The inclusion of such claims in the inventory therefore raises a number of thorny problems. As discussed later in this book, to some extent these problems are addressed by putting in place a settlement grid that will dictate whether a claimant receives compensation and, if so, how much, depending on a variety of predetermined criteria. Such settlement grids may provide plaintiffs with at least the appearance of objectivity and equal treatment. Nonetheless, problems may still arise in the proper allocation of funds, or at least plaintiff perceptions regarding whether the funds were allocated properly.

The failure to eliminate frivolous claims can also impede settlement efforts more generally. Defendants certainly do not want to pay for claims that lack merit. Where there is a failure to adjudicate cases in an MDL, or at least provide some level of scrutiny, there will be uncertainty in the minds of decision makers on the defense side concerning the quality of the inventory. Accordingly, there will be little appetite for throwing money at plaintiffs who have done little to nothing to prove the validity of their claims.

Some of this concern may be eliminated through the settlement structure. If a structure is put in place that includes stringent requirements before claimants receive compensation and any excess in settlement proceeds is returned to defendants, one would think some of defendants' concern would be mitigated. While scrutiny is not applied on the front end through normal litigation procedures, at least some level of scrutiny is applied at the back end.

However, the experience with such procedures has shown they do not fully mitigate the problems associated with a failure to weed out invalid claims before settlement. One example that has received widespread attention is the settlement in the *Propulsid* litigation. Propulsid was a popular heartburn medication that plaintiffs alleged caused a variety of heart irregularities. Litigation involving these personal injury claims was centralized in the U.S. District Court for the Eastern District of Louisiana before Judge Eldon Fallon. The parties developed a settlement agreement that established a panel of independent physicians who were jointly selected by the parties to review each claim. The experts determined whether, and to what extent, each of the claimants would receive compensation based on agreed-upon criteria.

However, when this review took place, a shockingly small percentage of the asserted claims satisfied the minimal criteria for compensation. Only 37 of 6,012 plaintiffs who chose to settle their cases survived this independent medical review and ultimately received compensation.[29] In contrast, the lawyers representing plaintiffs who brought the litigation received tens of millions of dollars. This result occurred because the lawyers' compensation was determined, at least in part, based on the face amount of the potential settlement. The expectation going in was that a greater percentage of the claims would survive the medical review and receive compensation. When this did not occur, there was a large gap between the compensation received by plaintiff counsel and the compensation received by plaintiffs themselves. The lead plaintiff counsel were awarded "over $27 million in common-benefit fees," while the plaintiffs themselves recovered only $6.5 million from the settlement fund.[30]

Commentators such as Professor Elizabeth Chamblee Burch sometimes cite the *Propulsid* settlement as an example of lawyers receiving a windfall at the expense of plaintiffs.[31] They suggest that the criteria for settlement plaintiff counsel negotiated were too stringent and the problem was not that the lawyers received compensation, but rather that the criteria to which they agreed unfairly barred the plaintiffs from receiving compensation. However, the criteria for assessing claims under the settlement agreement were negotiated in an arms-length manner and were fair. Moreover, they were implemented by independent medical professionals. Requiring that plaintiffs demonstrate they were exposed to a product and had a compensable injury as a result is not somehow inequitable. Moreover, requiring plaintiff evidence to survive independent scrutiny by medical experts is not unfair, particularly given that in the federal court system the Rules of Evidence specifically require scientific evidence to be both relevant and reliable to be admissible to prove a claim.[32]

Accordingly, what this episode really illustrates—in powerful fashion—are the pitfalls of trying to provide scrutiny to claims at the back end during the settlement process. This approach inevitably results in a windfall for plaintiff counsel. Indeed, in hindsight this result should not have been a surprise given the litigation history of the *Propulsid* MDL. During the MDL, a single bellwether case made it to trial, resulting in a defense verdict. The MDL court granted defendants summary judgment in the two other bellwether cases based on the lack of any reliable scientific evidence of causation, and consequently these cases never made it to trial.[33] Thus, even before the parties executed the settlement, there was anecdotal evidence that there could be significant problems with the viability of many of the claims in the litigation.

Nor is the result in the *Propulsid* litigation an aberration. Other MDL settlements have exhibited similar results. In the *Vioxx* litigation, for example, plaintiffs alleged that the arthritis pain killer Vioxx caused a variety of adverse cardiovascular events. The JPML established an MDL proceeding and there was prolonged litigation with multiple bellwether cases going to trial. However, once the case was settled, the data showed that a large segment of the plaintiff population (nearly 30 percent) could not establish basic elements of their claims, including that they had actually had Vioxx prescribed for them and had experienced an adverse cardiovascular event, such as heart attack or stroke, as a result.[34]

These examples appear to be in line with what is seen in mass tort MDLs more generally. While there is a lack of publicly available information regarding the outcomes of MDL settlements, those who represent defendants in multiple MDL proceedings, and who therefore should possess relevant information, have estimated that "approximately 30 to 40 percent of plaintiffs' claims are dismissed at the settlement stage."[35]

These figures demonstrate that, in many MDLs, the task of scrutinizing claims is pushed off to the settlement phase. At this point, the review may be relatively cursory. Most settlements do not involve the sort of independent medical review that occurred in the *Propulsid* litigation. As a result, claims that are not valid may receive compensation, potentially at the expense not only of defendants, but also other plaintiffs who have valid claims and could have bargained for increased compensation if the plaintiff population were smaller. Moreover, trying to determine which cases should receive compensation and in what amount at the settlement stage is an inherently flawed process that may lead to unjust outcomes. It is by definition more cursory and is characterized by a lack of transparency, given that the results of settlement allocations are rarely publicized. While the process certainly could be improved, potentially by requiring disclosure of settlement results, the administrative task of implementing a settlement generally will not match the adversarial process of actually litigating cases in court.

Failing to remove meritless claims can also have an adverse effect on the process of adjudication. First, and most obviously, the more cases filed in an MDL, the harder it is to resolve them. Most MDL proceedings lead to an inordinate amount of lawyer and judicial time expended in addressing cases that should not have been filed in the first place. Discovery must take place, information must be analyzed, and then the parties must spend time briefing and arguing dispositive motions. As a result, MDL proceedings typically last years and involve significant costs.

There are other less obvious ways in which a large number of meritless claims in the plaintiff population can interfere with adjudication of the cases. As discussed more fully later in this book, one way in which MDL courts have sought to get a handle on the potential value of claims is to hold trials over test cases, or bellwethers, so the parties may see how their arguments perform and what actual juries think regarding the value of the cases. The process of picking cases may vary from one MDL to another, but generally there is an attempt to pick representative cases that will give the parties an accurate look at the potential value of the claims. "If bellwether trials are to produce reliable information about the other cases in the MDL, the specific plaintiffs and their claims should be representative of the range of cases."[36] However, where the population of cases is filled with claims that lack merit and are therefore not representative of cases that might be eligible for compensation, the purpose of trying bellwethers is undermined.

Indeed, what typically happens when a case that lacks merit is selected through whatever procedures are put in place is that the plaintiffs voluntarily dismiss the case so it is not tried in order to avoid the significant chance of a defense verdict. Frequently, this is one of the turning points in an MDL proceeding where a judge who may not have a good understanding of the population of claims suddenly sees that there are potential problems with many of the cases.

Unfortunately, this realization often comes fairly late in an MDL proceeding. A relatively small percentage of cases out of the total population may be selected as bellwethers. Yet, the court may be faced with a situation where multiple bellwethers are voluntarily dismissed in the months leading to trial, which may be toward the end of the MDL proceeding.

While this phenomenon may provide an education for the MDL court, it can also significantly interfere with the bellwether process. The plaintiffs have the power to unilaterally skew the process by voluntarily dismissing potential bellwethers. As a result, the goal of representativeness is undermined, and the bellwether process becomes a less valuable tool in assessing the value of the asserted claims. Moreover, there is an inherent inconsistency in dismissing bellwethers that lack merit while keeping potentially thousands of other similarly non-meritorious cases in the MDL population.

While plaintiffs might argue that there is a countervailing mechanism available to defendants in the form of offering settlement to bellwether plaintiffs whose claims the defendants do not wish to try, this is a far less effective mechanism than that available to the plaintiffs. It depends on the willingness of the bellwether plaintiff to accept the settlement offer. If the bellwether plaintiff does not accept settlement, there is nothing defendants can do and they must try the case. Moreover, if a large settlement is offered it can become a potential marker or indicator of value for other claims, inflating the value of claims beyond what they are worth. Accordingly, the way the bellwether selection process currently functions, there is a significant potential for skewing the result toward the plaintiffs.

Conversely, some have argued that defendants have skewed the bellwether process through selective settlement of potential bellwether cases.[37] In her recent book, for example, Professor Burch points to the bellwether process in the *General Motors Ignition Switch* litigation as an example of this phenomenon. That litigation involved allegations that defective ignition switches in GM cars caused the engines to shut off while the vehicles were in motion. Among other criticisms of the bellwether process in the *Ignition Switch* MDL, Professor Burch notes that GM settled bellwether cases that might have been stronger trial candidates for the plaintiffs.[38] As a result, GM prevailed in the bellwether trials, which she believes significantly disadvantaged the plaintiffs in the MDL. Such settlements of potential bellwethers have occurred in other MDL cases. Nonetheless, as noted, the fact of settlement and the information it provides about the value of the claims may be similar to information provided by trying a bellwether case. If anything, the settlement might tend to overvalue the cases, given that defendants may be paying a premium for removing a potentially bad case (from their perspective) from the bellwether pool.

3
A Framework for Resolution

Despite the importance of weeding out claims in large MDL proceedings, the record in courts charged with doing so has been mixed. As noted, many cases result in settlements in which a large percentage of the asserted claims are not even eligible for compensation under the minimal requirements imposed by most settlement agreements. The experience with the administration of MDL settlements alone would suggest there is a fairly large deviation in the degree to which MDL courts have been successful in adjudicating the claims before them.

Many MDL courts have employed procedures to review the asserted claims efficiently and eliminate those that lack merit. At bottom, this is largely a matter of applying the normal rules of civil procedure in an MDL proceeding. These examples prove the point that courts presiding over MDL proceedings have the tools necessary to perform their jobs adequately. While courts have certainly developed a number of novel procedures that are somewhat unique to MDL proceedings, many of the courts that have been most effective in resolving cases have simply followed the normal rules of civil procedure.

However, when judges are confronted with thousands of asserted claims in an MDL proceeding, there is a temptation to engage in shortcut measures or broad-brush procedures that deviate from the normal rules and do not give adequate scrutiny to the cases that are filed. Judges may overestimate the amount of time it would take to consider and rule on issues raised by this volume of claims. While the resolution of common issues based on a single set of briefs may not be viewed as presenting a significant challenge, resolving case-specific issues is viewed as more time consuming. As a result, MDL courts may put these issues on the back burner or employ shortcut procedures that do not effectively resolve the claims. Cases that should be cleared out are allowed to linger on the docket, frequently awaiting an inevitable settlement where they may or may not be compensated.

As a practical matter, the burden is frequently on the defendants to raise these issues with the court and ask the court to employ the normal mechanisms available to adjudicate claims in an MDL proceeding. As the Panel has noted, "if defendants believe plaintiffs' counsel are filing frivolous claims, it is incumbent upon defense counsel to bring that concern to the attention of the transferee court, and to propose a process to identify and resolve such claims."[39]

Many judges who preside over MDL cases have never done so before, and even where they have, they may not be particularly familiar with the substance of the lawsuits.[40] More generally, there is frequently a process of education in which defendants must engage with the judge to present the basic facts regarding the case, the important issues the court must address, and procedures that may aid the court in addressing these issues in an efficient and effective manner. At the same time, plaintiffs must educate the court regarding their view of the case, and there is frequently a debate at the outset of the MDL regarding the procedures the court should employ and the schedule the court should follow in addressing the issues the parties raise.

Case Management

One of the primary challenges for the MDL court is the management of the sort of large-scale litigation typical of MDL proceedings. As the Federal Judicial Center has observed, "[m]ultidistrict litigation presents a federal judge with difficult management, intellectual, and personal challenges."[41] The court must first deal with the relatively mundane aspects of presiding over litigation before it resolves the merits of the cases before it. A variety of materials have been prepared by entities such as the Federal Judicial Center and Duke Law School's Bolch Judicial Institute in an effort to assist MDL courts in doing the basic work of managing the litigation. While the challenges of multidistrict litigation for the court and the parties should not be underestimated, at least some commentators argue that "most MDLs run extremely efficiently and smoothly from beginning to end."[42] Indeed, "[m]anaging an MDL fundamentally is no different from managing any other case, except that an MDL usually has the added complexity of more moving parts—lawyers, parties, jurisdictions, choice-of-law issues, varieties of discovery, and differentiated claims, just to mention a few."[43]

Despite these commonalities, the organizational challenges an MDL proceeding presents for the court can be significant. There may be thousands of claimants represented by many different law firms with their own perspectives and potentially divergent views about how to proceed. Moreover, these complexities may be compounded where there are related proceedings occurring in state courts in parallel with an MDL proceeding. Accordingly, it is important for the court to move quickly to establish a case-management plan for the MDL with the input of the parties.

In formulating a case-management plan, there are many different considerations an MDL court must keep in mind. For example, the Duke guidelines identify the following objectives that MDL courts should strive to meet in crafting a case-management order: "The objectives of an MDL proceeding should usually include: (1) the elimination of duplicative discovery; (2) avoiding conflicting rulings and schedules among courts; (3) reducing litigation costs; (4) saving the time and effort of the parties, attorneys, witnesses, and courts; (5) streamlining key issues; and (6) moving cases toward resolution (by trial, motion practice, or settlement)."[44]

To accomplish these and other goals, MDL courts have employed a number of case-management procedures. Typically, MDL courts seek to hold routine conferences and hearings with the parties to manage the litigation efficiently and address issues as they arise. Likewise, courts typically issue detailed orders governing various procedural matters in the case. In addition, many MDL courts utilize websites to publicize the court's orders and to keep the participants and other courts that may have related cases continuously informed regarding the proceedings.[45] Transparency and frequent engagement are important in managing the litigation.

In addition, early in the proceeding, courts endeavor to put in place a scheduling order that lays out the various events that will occur during the course of the MDL proceeding. According to the Federal Judicial Center, "[s]cheduling a prompt organizational conference sends a message that you are serious about organizing and moving the MDL."[46] MDL courts attempt to craft the order with the input of the parties so that it contains realistic deadlines for the basic events in the litigation.

Given the nature of the MDL proceedings, however, the scheduling order is necessarily a flexible document. MDL proceedings can last years and may involve thousands of participants. Accordingly, many unforeseen circumstances may occur that will require changes in the schedule. Indeed, sometimes MDL courts find it preferable to put in place only a partial schedule governing the initial phases of the proceeding. As the MDL proceeds, the court can then issue subsequent scheduling orders that govern future events in the litigation.

In crafting the scheduling order, the MDL court frequently obtains significant assistance from the parties. At the outset of the proceedings, the court obviously will not be as familiar with the nature of the litigation as the parties. Accordingly, it is not uncommon for the parties to submit proposed case-management orders and, indeed, the Federal Judicial Center recommends that before the initial conference the MDL court "require counsel to meet and confer with one another and submit a proposed initial case management order."[47]

Early implementation of a scheduling order is not only important to put in place a structure that will govern the proceedings, but it is also a good way for the court to begin to learn about the litigation. One of the ways the parties can assist the MDL court in learning about the litigation and in crafting the scheduling order is to identify "key issues that, if decided early or on an expedited basis, would speed settlement or other resolution of the litigation as a whole."[48] The parties can assist the court in crafting the schedule so the significant issues in the litigation can be addressed early in the proceedings. This will make the case progress more efficiently and may dispense with the need for the court and the parties to expend resources on other issues that may not be as important to making progress toward resolution of the litigation.

The role of the MDL court in this regard is similar to the role of federal courts in any civil case. Federal Rule of Civil Procedure

16 provides a source of guidance regarding pre-trial conferences and federal court scheduling orders, encouraging "early and continuing control" over the litigation.[49] The Federal Judicial Center's *Manual for Complex Litigation* recommends that, "[i]n early Federal Rule of Civil Procedure 16 conferences and status conferences, the judge and counsel should work to narrow the issues, claims and defenses."[50] In particular, the *Manual* observes that identifying such issues early in the litigation is "critical to developing a plan for efficiently resolving complex tort litigation."[51] In addition, Rule 16 specifically encourages courts presiding over federal litigation to use the pre-trial conference to, among other things, engage with the parties in "formulating and simplifying the issues, and eliminating frivolous claims or defenses."[52]

Over time, many circumstances will change in the MDL proceeding, which, in turn, may or may not warrant changes to the schedule. In a large mass tort litigation, for example, new plaintiffs may continue to file cases against the defendants in the MDL in different jurisdictions. The JPML may receive notice of these potential tag-along actions from the parties or from clerks where the cases are pending.[53] "'Tag-along' actions are those that appear to share common facts with the MDL actions already transferred."[54] When the JPML receives notice of a new filing, it prepares for transfer of the case to the court presiding over the MDL proceeding by issuing a conditional transfer order. Interested parties may object to transfer on the grounds that the case is not really related to the MDL and should not be transferred for consolidation. If there are objections, the Panel will resolve them and determine whether the case should be transferred to the MDL or should remain with the federal transferor court where the case is currently pending. Thus, during the course of a large MDL, one can expect there will be a continuous flow of additional cases transferred from other jurisdictions or filed directly with the MDL court.

As a result, the MDL court must determine how these additional tag-along cases are addressed. Typically, an MDL court will provide that rulings made by the MDL court before tag-along cases are transferred apply to the new cases, unless the parties object. In addition, discovery that has been taken will likewise be applicable in the new actions as they are transferred.[55] As the Federal Judicial Center has noted, “Ordinarily, it is advisable to order that (1) tag-along actions are automatically made part of the centralized proceedings upon transfer to, or filing in, the transferee court; (2) rulings on common issues—for example, on the statute of limitations—are deemed to apply to the tag-along action without the need for separate motions and orders; and (3) discovery already taken shall be available and usable in the tag-along cases.”[56] Accordingly, the flow of new tag-along cases rarely provides any significant disruption to the proceedings.

In conjunction with subsequent hearings after the initial scheduling conference, MDL courts frequently require the parties to provide routine status reports in advance of hearings that address matters such as new case filings, issues with ongoing discovery, the status of state court proceedings involving similar cases, and any other scheduling or administrative issues. These status reports provide an opportunity for the court to receive information regarding the parties’ activities since the last hearing and weigh in on any issues that require its attention.

Involvement of Third Parties

The court may also seek the assistance of third parties to make the proceedings more efficient. This may include magistrate judges or special masters who can assist with case management, resolve discovery disputes, or as we will see in subsequent chapters, make recommendations regarding rulings on the merits or facilitate settlement discussions. MDL courts may appoint special masters pursuant to their authority under Federal Rule of Civil Procedure 53: “Fed. R. Civ. P. 53 authorizes judges to appoint special masters to aid in handling pretrial matters ‘that cannot be effectively and timely addressed by an available district judge or magistrate judge of the district.’”[57] Where special masters are appointed, typically the costs are split among the parties.

Another type of third party that MDL courts sometimes employ is an independent expert. While infrequent, some courts have utilized independent experts to assist them in understanding complex scientific or technical issues raised in the litigation. In the *Breast Implant* MDL, for example, the court appointed a panel of independent experts to assess the reliability of scientific evidence that plaintiffs maintained showed that silicone breast implants cause disease. The opinions of these experts subsequently were cited in decisions excluding contrary opinions asserting there was such a link.[58] The Federal Rules of Evidence contain provisions specifically authorizing such appointments: "Testifying expert witnesses may be appointed under Fed. R. Evid. 706. Non-testifying technical advisors may be appointed under the court's broader inherent authority to invite expert assistance in duties necessary to decide a case."[59]

In some proceedings, use of magistrates or special masters may have benefits, especially where the MDL involves a large number of claims or where such third parties have particular expertise that may be relevant to the proceedings. For example, a special master with expertise in electronic discovery who has worked in prior MDL proceedings may bring knowledge or experience that can increase the efficiency of an MDL proceeding. The special master can handle complicated technical issues as they arise, while allowing the MDL judge to focus on more substantive matters. Similarly, there may be special masters who have particular expertise in facilitating settlement discussions, allowing the MDL judge to avoid becoming involved in such negotiations. This may add value to the MDL proceeding by avoiding unnecessary recusal or perceptions of unfairness, to the extent the MDL judge is privy to information derived from the settlement negotiations the parties would not otherwise disclose to the court.

Commentators have noted, however, that there are trade-offs inherent in the use of third parties and magistrates, including cost and a potential reduction in engagement by the MDL judge in the day-to-day management of the proceedings: "The use of magistrate judges and special masters may be critical to avoiding delays in addressing time-consuming matters, such as disputes over privileged-document designations or technical electronic discovery issues. However, the court should avoid over-delegation, as it can make management and coordination more difficult and add unduly to the parties' expenses."[60] In addition to reducing the MDL judge's involvement in the proceeding, the use of magistrates or special masters may lead the parties to lodge objections if they view the process as less efficient or if they are not inclined to have third parties involved. Accordingly, there are a variety of reasons that over-utilization of special masters or magistrates should be avoided.

Moreover, the parties may raise additional concerns with respect to the use of special masters or independent experts who are not employed on a permanent basis by the federal courts. For example, where the third party is a private special master, the parties may have to bear costs they would otherwise not incur. In addition, there may be questions about whether the special master is more inclined to favor one side or the other. This may be particularly true in certain types of MDL proceedings. As the Federal Judicial Center has noted, "[i]n a products liability MDL, it may be particularly difficult to appoint a completely disinterested special master with no prior relationship to any of the parties, since special masters are often practicing attorneys and tend to have substantial experience with similar disputes."[61]

Special masters in MDL proceedings are often repeat players who may have interacted with the same lawyers in other MDL cases and whose incentives may be shaped by a desire to continue receiving similar work in the future. In contrast, magistrate judges are funded by the courts and thus such questions may not arise: "Appointment of a magistrate judge as a special master makes it unnecessary to worry about imposing extra expense on parties or about the question of neutrality."[62]

While the parties may have no choice but to turn over certain aspects of the case to a magistrate, they may not wish to relinquish the degree of control that occurs when issues are turned over to private third parties such as special masters and independent experts. Indeed, some commentators have noted that the use of repeat players as special masters may introduce a bias into the process that tends to disadvantage some plaintiffs and plaintiff lawyers who are not among the leadership in an MDL proceeding.[63] The concern is that repeat player plaintiff and defense counsel may support the appointment of a small group of individuals who regularly serve as special masters in large MDL proceedings. These individuals then have an incentive to act in the interests of the lead lawyers, potentially at the expense of plaintiff counsel who are not appointed to leadership committees. Whether or not such biases manifest themselves, there is always the possibility that appointment of a special master may lead to objections by participants in the MDL process and may be a source of further contention during the proceedings.

Finally, the use of court-appointed experts may raise additional concerns. The parties frequently will find it preferable to present their own experts to the court on scientific or technical issues and to exclude other, potentially conflicting voices that the court may have a natural tendency to favor. Adding an independent expert to the mix introduces a significant level of uncertainty. Moreover, questions may arise regarding the degree to which the parties can cross-examine the independent expert or obtain discovery regarding the expert's methodology. Accordingly, there are significant procedural questions that may be raised by the introduction of independent experts.

Moreover, when a federal court appoints its own independent experts, it represents a move away from the normal adversarial process that is the model in the United States. Unlike Europe, where judges may take a more active role as factfinders, in the United States we generally leave it to the parties and the lawyers to develop the facts and arguments, which are then presented to the court. The court acts as a neutral decision maker based on the facts and arguments presented to it. Introducing independent experts who may have a role in either fact development or in influencing decision making represents a deviation from this traditional model.

Coordination of Plaintiff Counsel

One of the issues a court must confront in any MDL proceeding is the fact that, because there may be thousands of cases consolidated before the court, there will inevitably be numerous law firms representing plaintiffs with different ideas about how their cases should proceed. There is therefore a need for some means of coordination among plaintiff counsel. While many of these lawyers may simply be along for the ride and have no desire to be actively involved in the proceedings, many others will have a strong desire to participate and strong views about how the cases should be litigated.

While such issues regarding coordination are frequently much less significant on the defense side, there may also be challenges regarding coordination among defendants. In a large MDL proceeding there can be multiple defendants who may have different interests and views about how to try the cases. While there are typically far fewer participants on the defense side, and coordination typically functions much better without the need for any judicial intervention, the MDL court may also face some issues with coordination among defendants.

MDL courts have developed procedures to address these coordination issues and provide a formal framework for participation by the lawyers, particularly on the plaintiff side. One of the first actions of the MDL court generally is to establish leadership committees and select plaintiff counsel to serve on those committees: "Early organization of the counsel who have filed the various cases is a critical case-management task."[64] In smaller MDLs, there may only be a single committee. However, there has been a trend in MDL cases toward establishing multiple committees with different functions. This allows a greater number of firms to participate in the litigation and increases the diversity of plaintiff counsel actively involved in the litigation.

One of the functions of the leadership committees is to perform much of the actual work that occurs in the litigation. However, the leadership is also responsible for providing funding to pursue the litigation. Accordingly, there is a tendency to appoint well-funded, repeat-player plaintiff firms that have served on committees in other MDL proceedings.

Typically, an MDL court will establish a steering or executive committee to lead the litigation. However, as noted, the court may appoint additional committees to carry out the work in the litigation. For example, MDL courts may establish committees charged with conducting discovery, developing expert evidence, or researching the law and drafting motions. The greater the number of committees, the greater the possibility that coordination among counsel may be more unwieldy. At the same time, however, a greater number of committees also expands opportunities for participation in the work of the MDL.

Which plaintiff firms serve on these committees is often a hotly contested issue. Not only does service on the committees represent an opportunity to control the litigation, but the law firms serving on these committees often receive significantly greater compensation. MDL courts typically establish a common benefit fund to pay the law firms for their work on these committees.[65] The common benefit fund comprises monies derived from trials or settlements in the MDL. While there is a delay in the receipt of such funds, which are paid when the litigation concludes, they can be significant for the lawyers who receive them, given that they are frequently derived from an assessed percentage applied to all compensation plaintiffs receive in the litigation: "Membership on the steering committee entails an enormous amount of work, but it can come with a huge payoff—certainly larger than the contingency fee expected from representing one or even several individual plaintiffs—because attorneys who do work for the common benefit of the group typically receive a portion of every single plaintiff's payoff."[66] Accordingly, members of the plaintiff's bar have significant incentive to attempt to be appointed to these committees.

An MDL court also has an interest in the selection process. The court has an interest in appointing counsel who are competent, hardworking, and can get along with other plaintiff firms to avoid problems during the course of the MDL. It also has an interest in ensuring that the lawyers who are appointed to the committees have the time and commitment necessary to carry out their responsibilities, as well as the resources necessary to fund the litigation. In sum, the course of the MDL can be shaped to some extent by the initial decision of whom to appoint to these plaintiff committees.

In many MDLs, plaintiff firms attempt to coordinate with each other before the decision is made to present the court with a slate of agreed-upon candidates. This process typically reinforces a pattern where the same plaintiff firms serve on committees in multiple MDLs. Despite such coordination, however, there will always be firms excluded from this process that may seek representation on the committee, or the MDL court itself may seek to go beyond merely rubber stamping a proposed slate of candidates presented to it by the plaintiff's bar. Accordingly, there is room for new representation on these committees, and MDL courts increasingly endeavor to expand the number of lawyers serving on the committees.

MDL courts typically "audition" plaintiff firms for spots on the committees, soliciting applications and presiding over a hearing during which the court can observe the individual lawyers who are seeking to serve on the committees and hear their arguments in support of their applications: "Many judges request that lawyers submit their resumes, descriptions of their prior experience in other complex litigation, and their proposed fee arrangements."[67] A hearing on the applications gives the court an opportunity to further familiarize itself with the lawyers who apply to serve on the committees. The court may also seek the views of other MDL judges who have experience with the lawyers who are applying in order to solicit their opinions. According to one source, "[t]he judge's primary responsibility in the selection process is to ensure that the lawyers appointed to leadership positions are capable and experienced and that they will responsibly and fairly represent all plaintiffs, keeping in mind the benefits of diversity of experience, skills, and backgrounds."[68]

Despite an MDL court's best efforts, however, there may be conflict within the leadership team and between the leadership team and the rest of the lawyers representing plaintiffs in the MDL proceeding. Members of the leadership team are likely experienced lawyers with strong personalities who have their own views regarding how the litigation should proceed. Accordingly, in order for the MDL to function smoothly, it is important that the lawyers on the committees work cooperatively with each other. Potentially of greater consequence are conflicts between members of the leadership committee and the other plaintiff counsel in the litigation. The interests of these two groups are not always aligned. There may be lawyers who are not serving in leadership positions who believe the leaders are not acting in the best interest of the plaintiffs as a whole. Conversely, leadership may believe that lawyers not on the committees are free-riding off leadership efforts and that they may not even be undertaking basic work necessary to adequately screen their own cases before filing them. Indeed, as we shall see, there have been examples where disputes between the two groups have become significant and public, leading to disruptions of the MDL proceeding. MDL courts, aware of the importance of working cooperatively with other lawyers representing plaintiffs, take this into account in determining membership on leadership committees. A cooperative relationship among members of the committees, as well as between the committees and the other lawyers representing plaintiffs in the litigation, is important for the efficient resolution of the litigation.

Indeed, in part because of the potential for divergence of interests between lawyers on the committees and other lawyers representing plaintiffs in the litigation, some commentators have argued that the appointment of lawyers to serve on leadership committees raises due process concerns: "[N]either clients nor their attorneys freely consent to multidistrict litigation or the judge's choice for lead lawyers. This non-voluntariness makes the committee appointment more akin to choosing class counsel where absent class members have no say in who represents them."[69]

Measures that may help avoid such conflicts include open and frequent communication with lawyers who are not serving on the leadership committees and allowing such lawyers to do work in the MDL. Open communication can avoid problems by providing the lawyers with ongoing information and allowing them to privately object or provide input on the leadership's approach if they are inclined to do so.

Permitting lawyers who are not on the leadership committees to do work in the MDL proceeding increases the sense of participation and buy-in among firms that are not members of the leadership committees. Some judges believe such participation should be actively encouraged: "[T]he transferee court can encourage the PSC to create subcommittees comprised of interested plaintiff attorneys not on the PSC and assign these attorneys tasks consistent with the duties of the PSC. The court should announce this policy in its minute entries, in open-court meetings, and on its MDL website and invite all plaintiffs' attorneys in the litigation who are interested in doing common benefit work to contact the PSC and coordinate their efforts through the PSC."[70]

In the event there are problems with firms serving on the leadership committees, another potential remedy available to the MDL court is to change the membership of the committees. In doing so, the court can remove lawyers who are not fulfilling their duties. Alternatively, even where there are no problems, the court can allow for greater participation in a lengthy MDL by rotating the membership of the committees to some extent over the course of the proceeding.

None of these are perfect solutions, and there inevitably will be some degree of conflict among the plaintiff firms involved in an MDL proceeding. The interests of the firms are not always aligned, and significant compensation may be at stake. Accordingly, one of the challenges courts presiding over MDL proceedings face is to monitor and potentially manage, to some extent, the relationships among firms participating in the proceedings: "A transferee judge should be alert throughout the MDL proceedings for potential and emerging disagreements and conflicts between lead and non-lead counsel."[71]

However, regardless of the conduct of the committees in the litigation, the fact remains that each plaintiff in an MDL proceeding continues to be represented by his or her own lawyer. While these lawyers may be hamstrung in some respects by the leadership structure, each case retains its own individual nature. Where case-specific issues are raised, for example, it is ultimately up to an individual plaintiff's counsel to respond to those issues on behalf of his or her client. Moreover, individual lawyers in the litigation retain the ability to make their views known regarding the conduct of the litigation, regardless of whether they are members of the leadership committees.

4
Discovery and Exchange of Information

After the MDL court establishes a leadership structure and a scheduling order that will frame the litigation, it may quickly turn its attention to the exchange of information by the parties through discovery. In particular, during the initial stages of the MDL, it is important for defendants to obtain basic information regarding the filed claims so they can review and evaluate the merits of those claims themselves. Accordingly, reflecting the general practice in MDL cases, independent guidelines like those issued by Duke Law School's Bolch Judicial Institute recommend early disclosure of basic information regarding the claims in an MDL proceeding: "At an early juncture, individual claimants should be required to produce information about their claims."[72]

As the guidelines explain, such early disclosure is not unusual in civil litigation, regardless of whether cases are part of an MDL proceeding. Rather, such disclosure occurs all the time in normal civil cases filed on an individual basis in the federal courts. The procedure in an MDL proceeding should be no different; indeed, in an MDL, it is particularly important to ensure that "both sides obtain information critical to claims or defenses."[73]

As the guidelines observe, in an MDL proceeding there may be additional reasons to ensure there is early disclosure. The facts obtained through disclosure may be particularly relevant in selecting test cases during the bellwether process that typically occurs in a large MDL proceeding. It also may be important in efforts to achieve a settlement of the claims. Absent good information about the entire universe of claims, it is difficult for the parties to agree on a negotiated resolution. Finally, as the guidelines acknowledge, there is a particular concern in MDL proceedings with the filing of meritless claims: "requiring plaintiffs at an early juncture to produce information verifying their basic factual allegations addresses concerns that MDL proceedings invite unsubstantiated claims."[74] In sum, requiring early disclosure of facts supporting the claims is critical to making progress in the litigation.

Streamlined Procedures for Discovery

Accordingly, MDL courts have developed streamlined procedures to assist with the discovery process. Courts presiding over large MDLs frequently require the parties (particularly plaintiffs) to fill out fact sheets that identify basic facts critical to evaluating the claims, as well as the production of basic information such as medical records that would be relevant to issues such as causation and product identification in a product liability case. As the Duke guidelines note, such early disclosure has become a best practice because the information disclosed is important for multiple reasons, including case management, selecting potential test cases for trial, and settlement negotiations.

Most obviously, "[f]act sheets also help to uncover cases that should not have been centralized in the first instance."[75] "They . . . can provide an efficient mechanism to assist the parties and the court in assessing whether certain claims may be candidates for expedited resolution through voluntary withdrawal, dispositive motions, or through a settlement process."[76] Simply requiring production of basic information can frequently lead to the prompt elimination of claims that are unsupported. In many instances it will quickly become apparent whether a claim can proceed based on basic documents relating to the claims or answers to basic questions regarding fundamental elements necessary to prove the claims.

Developing the fact sheet is usually a matter of negotiation among the parties. Each MDL proceeding is unique and, to some extent, the particular facts and circumstances of the case will drive the information required in the fact sheet and the documents requested. However, in large mass tort cases there are certain standard questions regarding the plaintiff's alleged injury, use of the product, and damages that may carry over from proceeding to proceeding. In sum, there is a body of standard questions on which the parties may draw in developing the fact sheet.

Nonetheless, each MDL is unique, and the particular facts and circumstances of each case will necessitate that certain specific requests be incorporated into the fact sheet. Thus, the development of the fact sheet early in the proceedings again underscores the need for the parties to familiarize themselves with the cases promptly so they will be in a position to request the information they need to defend the claims. Not only is the information critical in developing a schedule for the MDL and for communicating with the MDL judge, but quite quickly in the proceedings the parties will be asked to identify the basic information they believe they will need to litigate the claims.

This initial disclosure of information typically goes a long way toward identifying the claims that should not proceed. In a product liability case, for example, the plaintiff will be required to provide authorization to obtain the plaintiff's medical records. These records may tend to support or refute the plaintiff's individual claim, and in many cases it will be apparent from the face of these records whether the plaintiff's claim can proceed. While fact sheets filled out by the plaintiffs often contain errors or are incomplete, the basic documents that accompany the fact sheets are frequently dispositive.

The cost of collecting and going through these documents may be significant, however, and is a frequent bone of contention for defendants in an MDL. As we will see, various proposals have been suggested to reform MDL procedures so that the burden of identifying information that supports the plaintiffs' claims is shifted more toward the plaintiffs and away from defendants. Right now, it is often up to the defendants to go through the records and identify documents that potentially refute the plaintiffs' claims. This is particularly frustrating in MDL cases where plaintiffs file a high percentage of cases that lack merit.

Reform of this system is possible without formal amendment of rules or statutes. The court can accomplish some rebalancing through its authority over case management. For example, MDL courts may wish to consider potential cost-sharing measures, particularly where an initial review demonstrates that there are many claims in the inventory that are not valid. Likewise, the court can shift costs by imposing monetary sanctions in the event that plaintiff counsel have filed frivolous claims.[77]

Adding to this burden, in some MDL cases the court may require defendants to file fact sheets themselves, disclosing whatever information they have that may relate to each plaintiff's claims. However, these defendant fact sheets frequently are not that helpful in resolving claims. Information regarding the validity of plaintiffs' claims is, not surprisingly, largely within the plaintiffs' possession or in the possession of their health-care providers. Defendants rarely have information relevant to the individual claims.

Plaintiffs may push for such fact sheets largely in an attempt to impose costs on the defendants or in a desperate effort to come up with something they may use to avoid dismissal. Accordingly, there are cases in which plaintiffs have asked courts to consider requiring defendant fact sheets that provide all information the defendant might have regarding each plaintiff's claim. In a pharmaceutical product liability case, for example, a defendant manufacturer may have received an adverse event report relating to the plaintiff's condition. Likewise, plaintiffs sometimes seek to discover information regarding the relationship, if any, between a pharmaceutical company and the plaintiff's physician.[78] However, any information from an adverse event report is unlikely to go beyond the information contained in a plaintiff's own medical records, and information regarding any relationship between the plaintiff's physician and the defendant manufacturer will rarely be relevant to initial dispositive motions or other means of assessing the validity of claims.

Accordingly, even those sources that suggest consideration of defendant fact sheets recognize that they will not be appropriate in many cases and that an assessment must be made to determine their relevance. As the Duke guidelines note, for example, "[t]he utility and practicability of individualized information in defendant fact sheets depends upon a number of factors, including the nature of plaintiffs' allegations, the pre-suit relationship (if any) between plaintiffs and defendant, any contacts or relationship between defendant and plaintiffs' physicians, the likelihood of defendant possessing plaintiff-specific documents or information, and the accessibility and potential relevance of any such documents or information."[79] In the ordinary case, the availability, accessibility, and potential relevance of such documents will be low.

While such streamlined procedures have been developed in MDL proceedings to provide basic information to the parties at an early stage in the proceedings, that does not mean such streamlined procedures should supplant the normal rules governing discovery or that such streamlined procedures will be used in every MDL proceeding. Rather, these procedures typically supplement the normal rules of civil procedure, which allow the parties to seek information from the opposing side through a variety of means, such as document requests, requests for admission, interrogatories, and depositions, among other things. The Federal Rules of Civil Procedure apply equally to MDL proceedings, just as they would in an individual civil case filed in federal court.[80] Accordingly, all of the traditional tools of discovery are available to parties participating in MDL proceedings, and it is important those tools be utilized in situations where streamlined procedures do not provide sufficient information to adequately assess the validity of asserted claims.

Alternatively, parties in MDL proceedings may simply rely on the Federal Rules of Civil Procedure. The Duke guidelines, for example, note that, "[a]n alternative to fact sheets is standardized interrogatories or document requests."[81] Such standardized requests may be followed up in individual cases with additional more case-specific requests where necessary to obtain information needed to assess the validity of the individual claims. The federal rules provide established mechanisms that may be used to facilitate the exchange of information and, indeed, may be more appropriate, particularly in smaller MDL proceedings.

After the parties have disclosed initial, basic information about the claims, depending on the circumstances of the litigation, as a practical matter it may fall to the defendants to shoulder the burden of selecting and proposing procedural mechanisms to adjudicate the claims in the MDL. As we will see in subsequent chapters, there are a variety of procedures that may be utilized to evaluate the claims filed in an MDL proceeding. In some instances, the judge presiding over the MDL may have certain views regarding the procedures he or she would like to employ and may feel knowledgeable enough regarding the nature of the litigation to provide guidance regarding the procedural framework. However, the selection of the procedural framework frequently occurs early in the proceedings, when the judge is not as knowledgeable about the nature of the litigation. Accordingly, it frequently falls to the parties to suggest a procedural framework for the resolution of claims.

Litigants may seek to engage in this process of judicial education in a variety of ways. The most obvious way is to attempt to work in points regarding the merits in each filing with the court or appearance at a hearing. MDL proceedings typically have regular status hearings where matters regarding discovery and scheduling are discussed. These hearings can provide a good opportunity for the parties to work in some discussion of the merits of the cases. For example, the information that is sought in discovery obviously has relevance to the merits of the claims. To the extent there are disputes about certain aspects of discovery, it provides an opportunity for the parties to educate the court about why the discovery is relevant and the particular points the parties intend to make regarding the validity of the claims.

Likewise, deficiencies in plaintiffs' compliance with discovery requests can illustrate the problems with the asserted claims. For example, the fact sheets plaintiffs are required to complete in a product liability MDL may request basic information regarding plaintiffs' claims, such as the date of purchase of a particular product, the particular injuries that plaintiffs maintain they suffered and when those were diagnosed, and in some instances, identification of the documents in the record that support these basic facts. Inevitably, many plaintiffs in an MDL proceeding will not complete this basic information or will not do so in a timely fashion, either because they cannot do so without exposing that their claims lack merit or because they are not willing to do the most basic work to prosecute their claims. This stage in an MDL proceeding can provide the court with an early indication of whether there are potential problems in the inventory of claims. If a large percentage of the plaintiff population cannot comply with the most basic court orders to produce information supporting their claims, then it is likely there are significant problems with the claims that have been filed in the MDL proceeding.

Accordingly, thought must be given to what will happen if there is a lack of compliance with the fact sheet requirement. Somewhat surprisingly, noncompliance is not uncommon: "[T]here have been reported opinions in the largest mass-tort MDLs, usually involving allegedly harmful pharmaceuticals or medical devices, in which large numbers of fact sheets have been submitted with material, inaccurate information."[82] Plaintiffs frequently fail to submit completed fact sheets and sometimes fail to submit fact sheets at all. Such failure to prosecute the claims is a basis for elimination of the claims entirely. Moreover, in many instances it likely reflects the fact that, if the fact sheets were completed, it would quickly become apparent that the plaintiff has no viable claim. Dismissal for noncompliance with the fact sheet requirement is the approach recommended in various guidelines, which note the importance of enforcing deadlines for the submission of information to keep the MDL moving forward and progressing.

The question is whether the courts will offer plaintiffs a second chance or immediately proceed to eliminate the claims. As long as requirements are communicated in advance, the most appropriate approach may be to make clear to plaintiffs that failure to complete a fact sheet will be grounds for dismissal. While there may be some cases in which plaintiffs' failure to fill out a fact sheet may be excused based on a showing of good cause, to move the MDL along and avoid providing an incentive for plaintiffs to be less than diligent in complying with the court's orders, normally such noncompliance should be grounds for dismissal.

In some cases, there may be grounds for requiring the submission of very specific fact sheets tailored to important issues in the case. For example, the Duke guidelines suggest that product identification may be an issue that warrants a separate disclosure sheet in product liability MDLs.[83] Where, for example, there is a suspicion that lawyers have not been diligent about ensuring that each plaintiff was actually exposed to a particular product, it may be appropriate to have them fill out a separate fact sheet focused on this issue.

A good example of such a specific case-management order was issued in the *Taxotere (Docetaxel) Products Liability* litigation. That MDL involved allegations that a chemotherapy drug caused permanent hair loss. "Recognizing the importance of determining product identification," the court issued a specific order requiring plaintiffs to produce basic information that proved they received the product at issue in the litigation.[84] Specifically, the order required that plaintiffs identify the facility or hospital where they obtained the drug, specify the time frame of administration, and request and pay for medical, pharmacy, or billing records that contained proof of administration. The order also required the plaintiff to follow up with the facilities within 30 days if no records were obtained and, if the facilities did not voluntarily provide records, to issue a subpoena. Once the information was obtained, the order provided that: "Plaintiff shall voluntarily dismiss any and all named Defendants not identified by the Product ID Information."[85] If the plaintiff failed to dismiss a case lacking such evidence, then the defendant could place the issue on the agenda for the regular status meetings without having to file a formal motion to dismiss. Likewise, if the plaintiff failed to comply with the requirements of the product identification order, the plaintiff's claim was subject to dismissal.[86]

Such an order arguably preserves the normal burden in civil litigation that requires plaintiffs to produce evidence to prove each element of their claims. In this case, because product identification was likely to be a central issue in the case, the court put in place specific procedures to address this issue as a threshold question. In the absence of such an order, the burden may effectively shift to the defendants to collect and review the plaintiff's medical and billing records. Such a process can be relatively expensive. Accordingly, orders like the one in *Taxotere* help to ensure costs are not improperly shifted onto defendants. Moreover, they illustrate how basic documents in a product liability case can be used to eliminate unsupported claims in a very efficient manner. Whether the plaintiffs are effectively charged with undertaking this process, as under the order in *Taxotere*, or the defendants receive such documents or authorization to obtain such documents along with the plaintiff fact sheets, typically many claims in a product liability MDL can be resolved through a review of a discrete set of basic documents.

Phased Discovery and Other Modifications to the Discovery Schedule

In addition to providing for the collection of such basic information, the court must adopt procedures that will efficiently adjudicate the asserted claims. These procedures can then be incorporated into the scheduling orders entered at the beginning of the MDL proceeding. A standard scheduling order will provide for a period of discovery, including the submission of reports by experts for both sides, and deadlines for the filing of motions to dismiss and for summary judgment. However, there can be other procedures that result in the resolution of asserted claims that can be incorporated into the scheduling order. For example, as we have seen, there may be deadlines for completion of fact sheets and curing deficiencies in the fact sheets followed by dismissal for noncompliance. Likewise, as we will see in subsequent chapters, other procedures, such as *Lone Pine* orders, requiring the submission of independent medical opinions supporting the claims, magistrate review, or other procedures for scrutinizing the claims may be incorporated into the scheduling order.

Accordingly, from the outset of the proceedings it is important to have an understanding of the key issues that must be resolved in the litigation and proposals for procedures to resolve those issues. The process of drafting the scheduling order can be another vehicle for educating the court regarding the merits of the asserted claims and the sorts of issues the defendants plan to raise in seeking to invalidate the claims.

Moreover, the nature of the issues in the case can have a profound effect on the scheduling of an MDL proceeding. For example, the court may want to consider phasing discovery so the parties exchange certain discovery that is particularly relevant to early motions during an initial phase, followed by any remaining discovery in a subsequent phase, if necessary. In many cases, issues of causation and the reliability of scientific evidence are at the forefront of an MDL proceeding. These issues typically turn on publicly available scientific literature and perhaps internal studies a company has performed on its products. Discovery in cases raising such issues can be phased so that documents relating to early dispositive motions addressing these issues can be provided first, and then additional discovery is provided only if the early motions do not result in dismissal of the claims. Such procedures can help save the parties unnecessary time and expense. In the event early dispositive motions are granted, the parties can appeal any such rulings having saved the time and expense of completing discovery. In the event the motions are denied, the parties can pursue the remaining discovery in the ordinary course.

Another area in which such phased discovery may be appropriate is where defendants have significant arguments that federal law preempts the claims. The Supreme Court has held that, where state law tort claims conflict with federal law, the claims must be dismissed. Thus, for example, where the plaintiffs in a pharmaceutical product liability case allege that additional warnings should have been included in the product labeling, yet the U.S. Food and Drug Administration (FDA) has rejected such warnings as unnecessary or inappropriate, the claims are preempted by federal law that allows the FDA to regulate the content of such warnings. The Supreme Court recently held that the preemption issue is one that should be decided by judges, not juries, based on the regulatory record.[87] Accordingly, it is an issue that lends itself toward phasing of discovery. Many of the documents necessary to rule on the preemption issue will likely be a matter of public record. However, to the extent a defendant has material non-public documents, they can be produced in an initial phase of discovery, after which the court can decide whether the claims are preempted.

Such procedures have been effective in large MDL proceedings. The court in the *Incretin Mimetics* MDL issued such an order to phase discovery relating to certain threshold issues at the outset of the proceedings.[88] The *Incretin Mimetics* MDL involved claims that certain diabetes medications were associated with pancreatic cancer. The FDA indicated it did not believe there was sufficient scientific evidence to demonstrate a causal relationship or warrant any additional warning in the labeling regarding pancreatic cancer. Defendants sought an early ruling granting them summary judgment on the ground that the claims were preempted by the FDA's statements. Later, defendants also argued that even if the claims were not preempted, the court should grant summary judgment because there was no reliable scientific evidence demonstrating the medications were capable of causing pancreatic cancer.

The court granted the defendants' request for phased discovery, concluding that the court could take up the preemption issue in an initial phase that involved discovery only of core regulatory materials. Accordingly, defendants were able to limit production in this initial phase while they litigated the preemption issue. The court later provided for a period of discovery that would address the general causation issues, which entailed discovery of the parties' causation experts, followed by dispositive motions on these scientific issues. Thus, because these issues were central to the litigation, the court focused its efforts on their resolution.

Finally, the presence of class complaints may also warrant phased discovery or, at a minimum, some sort of accommodation in the schedule. According to the Federal Judicial Center: "Many MDLs involve overlapping statewide and national class actions. Sequencing the discovery and briefing necessary to resolve class certification and summary judgment motions is one of [the] most vital early tasks [in an MDL]."[89] Discovery relating to whether to certify a class obviously will overlap to some extent with discovery into the merits.[90] Nonetheless, much of the merits discovery may not be particularly relevant to class certification. Likewise, class certification may entail different sorts of discovery that would not occur in the absence of class allegations, such as discovery of the purported class representatives and potentially experts whose focus is tailored toward class certification. It may make sense to push off class certification issues or resolve them promptly, depending on the nature of the MDL proceedings and how significant class certification is to the nature of the claims. Accordingly, thought must be given to the presence of such claims in an MDL proceeding and provisions that may be incorporated into the court's scheduling order to accommodate them.

For example, in the *Meridia* MDL, plaintiffs filed several class actions that were put on the back burner while the parties litigated general causation issues. In *Meridia*, plaintiffs alleged that a weight-loss medication caused various adverse cardiovascular events, such as heart attacks and strokes. Plaintiffs filed thousands of individual personal injury actions alleging such injuries from taking the drug. In addition, however, some plaintiffs filed class actions seeking to represent classes of those who allegedly suffered personal injuries.

The court determined it would focus first on the issue of general causation before it determined whether to certify a class. Accordingly, the court ruled on motions for summary judgment and to exclude plaintiffs' expert evidence regarding causation first. The court ended up granting summary judgment and disposed of the litigation.[91] While there were some depositions of the class representatives before this ruling, by pushing off the issue of class certification the court avoided work that would have been unnecessary to the resolution of the claims.

Phasing discovery can be particularly beneficial for defendants in large MDLs because there is some degree of asymmetry between plaintiffs and defendants in terms of discovery in such MDL proceedings. In the typical product liability MDL, the defendants face far more significant discovery obligations than the plaintiffs. They are generally large corporations with records that may go back decades in some cases. In addition, electronic discovery can frequently be costly and a significant burden. Accordingly, where appropriate, it may make sense to look for opportunities to phase discovery sought from the defendants.

Indeed, independent guidelines and the Federal Judicial Center's *Manual for Complex Litigation* recommend that courts look for such opportunities. As the Duke guidelines note, "in many cases, the court and parties find phased production efforts preferable." As the guidelines explain, "'transferee judges frequently adopt staggered discovery plans that appear to both prioritize discovery into core matters and relevant matters that can be easily identified, retrieved, and produced first and allow for adaptation in future stages to account for discoveries in earlier stages.'" "The failure to phase discovery in this manner may result in either needless and expensive discovery or insufficient discovery to support the schedule of other aspects of the MDL proceeding (e.g., dispositive motions, development of expert testimony)."[92]

Grappling with these sorts of issues is not unique to MDL proceedings. Any large proceeding involving multiple claims or lawsuits will confront similar challenges. Accordingly, the processes and procedures discussed in this book have relevance not only in MDL proceedings but also in other aggregated litigation. Indeed, many states have adopted procedures similar to MDLs for consolidating claims for pretrial proceedings and, in fact, it is not uncommon to have consolidated state proceedings occur in parallel with an MDL proceeding in federal court.[93] Similarly, even where such formalized mechanisms are not present, related claims may be sent to a single court, as is frequently the case with environmental or other types of litigation.

Conversely, aggregated proceedings outside of the MDL context can potentially provide guidance for MDL proceedings. For example, state court judges have developed innovative procedures to attempt to weed out claims that lack merit, rolling up their sleeves and working through asserted claims to ensure plaintiffs are committed to prosecuting the claims before them. Likewise, tort claims are aggregated in large mass tort bankruptcy proceedings where courts routinely resolve large numbers of claims in an efficient, almost administrative manner. Finally, some have suggested MDL courts should look to class action proceedings to improve the process by which settlements are crafted.[94] While commentators have noted that there may be problems in class action proceedings as well, some have maintained that, "the current practice of MDL actually makes the modern class action appear to be the pinnacle of procedural due process by comparison."[95] In class action proceedings, there are significant requirements to ensure that settlements meet the basic elements of due process, whereas in MDL proceedings the settlement process is largely unregulated. Moreover, in class actions there typically is some measure of phasing of discovery, with class discovery separated to some extent from discovery on the merits. Accordingly, ideas for innovation in MDL proceedings may come from a variety of sources.

That is not to say the application of innovative procedures governing discovery or other matters will always be the same in each MDL proceeding. As with any litigation, each MDL proceeding has certain unique aspects. The nature of the claims, the particular facts relevant to those claims, and the governing legal principles will vary from case to case. Accordingly, some degree of flexibility is necessary to adapt procedures to the unique circumstances of each case to achieve greater efficiency.

Crafting the Scheduling Order

Because of these dynamics, it is important for the parties to develop a plan early in the proceedings. Defendants must identify issues they want the court to resolve that may narrow the litigation. Conversely, there may be issues the plaintiffs believe should be at the forefront of the litigation that they may want to address before the merits are fully litigated. This can include issues that are common to all claims, such as general causation in a product liability case. It may also involve issues that are case-specific, such as whether a particular plaintiff was actually exposed to a particular product. Once these issues are identified and the procedures for resolving them are planned, the parties can then craft a discovery schedule that ensures the specific information necessary to resolve these issues is available at each stage of the proceedings.

Common issues are frequently resolved through generic or omnibus motions as to categories of claims. In contrast, as we will see, there are many different mechanisms available for eliminating claims on a case-by-case basis. Most effective MDLs have parallel tracks for addressing common issues and case-specific issues. The parties can go through the materials produced in each of the individual cases and identify potential problems at the same time that they prepare to litigate the common issues. In this way, progress is made on both fronts.

These pre-trial mechanisms can be combined with less traditional mechanisms for dispute resolution. For example, in many MDLs, courts set a schedule for test cases or bellwether trials. However, it is important not to skip over the pre-trial mechanisms for narrowing the litigation before employing such dispute resolution mechanisms. Bellwether trials are significantly less useful where pre-trial issues have not been adjudicated and cases that lack merit remain in the population of claims.

Thus, when crafting the scheduling order, it is important to consider such prudential concerns. It makes sense to ensure the schedule provides that important dispositive motions are resolved before the selection of bellwether cases so cases that fail at the pre-trial stage are not included as test cases. Otherwise, the parties will potentially waste significant time and effort working up cases that are going nowhere, when the bellwether process should be used to assess the cases that are viable and likely to proceed to trial. Similarly, the scheduling order should anticipate that the parties will be raising case-specific issues throughout the proceedings and should not focus solely on the common issues that must be litigated.

Finally, there may be situations in which not all of these tracks make sense in a particular MDL proceeding. For example, some commentators have argued that bellwether trials are fundamentally inconsistent with the statutory framework establishing MDLs, which refers to consolidation for pre-trial proceedings and does not appear on its face to contemplate that MDL courts will actually try cases. According to such critics, "it remains an open question whether trials are even a proper function of an MDL court."[96]

Moreover, there are circumstances in which bellwether cases may not provide useful information. For example, in proceedings where there is a large diversity among the cases in the population before the MDL court, it may be difficult—if not impossible—to find cases that will be representative. As the Duke guidelines note, the MDL court must determine, in consultation with the parties, "whether holding bellwether trials would advance the litigation": "Concerns continue to be expressed that some MDLs are best managed by focusing on the statutory mandate to conduct pretrial proceedings with an eye toward remand instead of holding bellwether trials and resolving by settlement within the MDL proceedings."[97] Accordingly, there may be circumstances in which the costs of the bellwether process outweigh the potential benefits.

In developing the schedule governing an MDL proceeding, it is necessary to ensure discovery proceeds so the parties have the information necessary to undertake these tasks by the deadlines laid out in the scheduling order. As noted, MDL courts typically require early disclosure of basic information using procedures that courts have developed beyond the normal federal rules. Courts typically require personal injury plaintiffs, for example, to authorize the disclosure of their medical records or actually produce medical records early in the proceedings and, in many instances, these records can shed significant light on the validity of claims. Whether a plaintiff was exposed to a particular product or has a viable claim of causation can often be determined from the medical records alone. In addition, however, the fact sheets courts typically require plaintiffs to complete in large MDL proceedings generally require the disclosure of basic information regarding plaintiffs' allegations, such as the date of injury, type of injury, and scope of exposure to the product at issue. As noted, the failure to comply with these requirements itself can be a basis for dismissal of claims. However, the information collected through these initial procedures also frequently leads to dismissal of claims where it is clear the plaintiff cannot establish one or more fundamental elements necessary for recovery.

These procedures, however, should not be viewed as a substitute for discovery under the federal rules. Rather, they were designed as a means for providing basic information early in the proceeding so that weak or invalid claims could be identified and eliminated. They are a means of supplementing the normal rules to further the efficient resolution of the proceedings. In many instances, at least a preliminary evaluation of claims in a personal injury case can be done simply by reviewing the plaintiff's medical records. Therefore, these initial procedures can have significant value in eliminating meritless claims.

It is important, however, that courts and parties not stop with these initial procedures. Rather, they should keep in mind that the normal rules of civil procedure continue to apply equally in an MDL proceeding. In our adversarial system, the best guarantee that the truth of the claims will be revealed is when opposing parties vigorously investigate and prosecute their arguments in support of, or against, the asserted claims. The initial procedures courts typically employ in MDL proceedings do not elicit all the facts necessary to evaluate the claims. There may, for example, be important facts supporting a statute of limitations defense demonstrating that the claims were not timely filed that may be in the possession of the plaintiffs themselves. There may be facts demonstrating that the plaintiffs or their doctors were aware of the alleged risks of the products and therefore cannot claim there was any lack of warning. In sum, much can be achieved in an MDL proceeding simply by following the normal rules of civil procedure.

An often-cited concern that sometimes leads to a reticence to follow the normal procedures is the time and effort required to do so. An MDL proceeding may involve hundreds or thousands of claims. Theoretically, conducting discovery and litigating each of the claims can consume a large amount of time. However, the MDL process inherently lends itself to achieving significant efficiencies. Once the parties begin to litigate individual cases and the court begins to issue rulings, the framework for resolving cases becomes clear. The parties can save themselves time and expense by foregoing litigation over issues the court has already decided in other cases. The parties quickly learn which way the court is leaning on such issues and can receive important guidance that would not otherwise be available if the cases were individually litigated before different judges.

There are also efficiencies for the court itself as it sees the same types of issues again and again in individual cases. With each case, the learning curve becomes less steep. Efficiencies can also be achieved in the amount of effort the court needs to expend in communicating its rulings to the parties. It is not necessary to provide extensive analysis of the same issue multiple times; indeed, in general, the Federal Judicial Center suggests that to streamline the process, MDL courts "[c]onsider issuing short rulings, which assume that the reader has knowledge of the underlying facts and legal issues and which simply state [the court's] holdings and the reasons for them."[98]

Moreover, in assessing the level of effort required to adjudicate individual claims in an MDL proceeding, one must also keep in mind that the potential alternative is the individual litigation of the claims in federal courts across the country. One cannot simply hope for settlement, particularly in the current environment where defendants are increasingly resolved that they will not settle simply to end the litigation, regardless of the merits of the cases. Federal courts are capable of resolving cases on an individual basis and do so every day. There is nothing inherently problematic about litigating individual cases in the context of an MDL proceeding and, indeed, as the architects of such proceedings contemplated, litigating individual cases before a single judge in an MDL proceeding has significant advantages over litigating individual claims before numerous federal judges.

The fact that resolving thousands of cases by issuing a single ruling on common issues that disposes of the entire litigation or encouraging a global settlement may be more efficient or represent less work for the court does not mean litigating cases individually in an MDL proceeding does not also achieve significant efficiencies. Litigating cases one-by-one before a single judge who becomes familiar with the issues in the litigation is more efficient than having multiple judges take the time to educate themselves about the same issues over and over again. Moreover, the MDL court is charged specifically with undertaking such efforts. There is no exclusion in the MDL statute for case-specific issues. In any event, as we will see in subsequent chapters, many MDL courts have effectively and efficiently addressed case-specific issues, demonstrating that this is an effective use of the MDL procedure for resolving large numbers of related claims.

5
Resolving Common Issues

One of the primary tasks in an MDL proceeding is to resolve significant pre-trial issues relating to the merits of the asserted claims. This may occur before discovery at the motion to dismiss stage or it may occur after discovery through summary judgment proceedings. Having collected information regarding the asserted claims, the parties and the court are in a position to determine which claims have merit and should proceed and which claims should be eliminated from the MDL proceeding. As the Supreme Court has recognized, the MDL statute itself expressly contemplates that the MDL judge will rule on dispositive pre-trial motions that may result in termination of the filed cases: "Congress anticipated that, during the pendency of pretrial proceedings, final decisions might be rendered in one or more of the actions consolidated pursuant to § 1407. It specified that 'at or before the conclusion of . . . pretrial proceedings,' each of the transferred actions must be remanded to the original district '*unless [the action] shall have been previously terminated*.'"[99]

The issues may be case-specific in nature, or they may be common issues among all or some subset of the claims. Resolution of such issues is critical in achieving progress in an MDL proceeding. As Judge Robreno has observed based on his experience in the *Asbestos* MDL proceeding, "[r]egardless of the amount of judicial effort and resources, unless the court establishes a toll gate at which entrance to the litigation is controlled, non-meritorious cases will clog the process."[100]

Consistent with the recognized need for early resolution of issues and the corresponding need for early disclosure in an MDL proceeding, guidelines issued by various organizations underscore the need for MDL courts to resolve motions filed by the parties promptly. For example, the Federal Judicial Center tells prospective MDL judges: "Your ultimate responsibility is to resolve pretrial issues in a timely and expeditious manner. The transferee judge supervises discovery; resolves important evidentiary disputes, class certification issues, and dispositive motions . . . ."[101] Similarly, the guidelines published by Duke Law School's Bolch Judicial Institute note that prompt resolution of motions is important not only in terms of actually resolving the claims filed in an MDL proceeding, but also in terms of laying the groundwork for settlement in the event there is one: "The transferee judge should endeavor to keep the MDL proceeding moving by promptly resolving pending motions. Clear, concise, and prompt resolution of motions allows counsel to advise their clients about risks and expectations and may bring about an expedient global resolution of the MDL."[102] Accordingly, there are multiple reasons MDL courts should endeavor to resolve motions relating to the merits of the asserted claims promptly.

The resolution of dispositive motions provides important guidance regarding which types of claims are viable and which are not. The sort of motion practice that occurs as a matter of course under the federal rules in any individual case filed in federal court also occurs in an MDL proceeding. Because multiple cases are at issue in an MDL, and because those cases share common issues, courts also hear omnibus or generic motions that seek to resolve issues common to a group, or all, of the asserted claims. Such motion practice therefore defines the scope of the liability and may assist the parties in making progress toward a negotiated settlement. However, while motions are the most common and obvious vehicle for resolution of issues in an MDL proceeding, as discussed in subsequent chapters, they are not the only mechanism. Courts have employed a variety of creative mechanisms to scrutinize claims filed in MDL proceedings and weed out claims that lack merit.

Scrutiny of Scientific Evidence

Realizing that increasingly there is a problem with the claims being filed in MDL proceedings, MDL courts arguably have become more receptive to granting omnibus motions as to categories of claims or all claims in MDL proceedings.[103] Recent decisions like those by the courts in the *Mirena*, *Lipitor*, and *Zoloft* litigation demonstrate this trend. These and other examples illustrate how courts have used generic motion practice to eliminate an entire MDL proceeding or significantly narrow the scope of an MDL proceeding, finding, for example, that there was no reliable scientific evidence demonstrating that the defendant's product was capable of causing the injuries alleged. Indeed, a recent survey by Professor Elizabeth Chamblee Burch indicates that a number of MDL courts have granted such omnibus motions.[104] While each MDL proceeding raises its own unique facts and circumstances, courts have applied such mechanisms to a range of diverse issues.

The *Lipitor* MDL provides one example. There, the plaintiffs alleged that a cholesterol-reducing medication increased the risk of developing Type 2 diabetes in patients who took the drug. Various doses of the medication were at issue, and the level of evidence of causation differed according to the dose a patient received. As with other MDLs involving pharmaceutical products, the patient population had a significant background risk of developing the disease at issue. It was not surprising that individuals who were taking medication to address their high cholesterol levels would go on to develop diabetes at some point in the future. There are common related risk factors, such as obesity, that may explain the development of both conditions.

Defendants moved for summary judgment on the issue of general causation, arguing there was no reliable scientific evidence demonstrating that the medication was capable of causing diabetes. The court agreed with the defendants' argument with respect to the lower doses of the medication taken by the vast majority of patients, finding that the claims were not based on "sufficient facts and data."[105] However, the court denied the motion with respect to the highest dose of the medication (80 mg).[106]

The *Lipitor* MDL therefore provides an illustration of a court significantly narrowing the scope of an MDL proceeding through generic motion practice. The court assessed the reliability of the expert opinions and scientific evidence submitted by the plaintiffs in the case, ruling on a motion under *Daubert v. Merrell Dow Pharmaceuticals* that determined the admissibility of the expert evidence. The court concluded that the expert causation evidence with respect to the lower doses was not sufficiently reliable to be submitted to the jury, and therefore excluded it. Absent such evidence, plaintiffs could not prove that the lower doses of Lipitor caused their injuries, and therefore summary judgment was warranted.

The *Lipitor* ruling illustrates how federal courts can effectively assess scientific evidence relating to generic issues such as causation and, in doing so, significantly narrow the scope of the litigation. Whereas in an individual case such rulings have effect only for that particular case, in an MDL proceeding the effect of such rulings is magnified because they effectively determine the outcome of a large group of claims. Thus, one way in which MDL courts can achieve significant efficiencies is by examining scientific evidence submitted on such common issues on a global basis.

A similar outcome occurred in the *Mirena* MDL proceeding. There, the MDL court likewise examined the scientific evidence regarding causation, but issued a much broader and sweeping ruling that effectively terminated the litigation. In *Mirena*, the plaintiffs alleged that an intrauterine birth control device (IUD) was defective, causing the device to embed in, or perforate, the uterus. Plaintiffs submitted the opinions of a variety of experts to support their allegations, which were based primarily on hypothesized mechanisms of action and studies in animals.

In a very expert-specific analysis, the court went through each of the experts' opinions and found them unreliable and therefore inadmissible, concluding that they did not "rise to the level of intellectual rigor employed in the medical or scientific field."[107] The court concluded that the experts' opinions were unsupported by adequate scientific evidence, were developed solely for the purpose of the litigation rather than through independent scientific inquiry, and that the theories the experts offered were flawed and unreliable. As in many other mass tort cases where plaintiffs have sought to rely on mechanism and animal evidence in lieu of reliable human studies demonstrating causation, the court found that plaintiffs' proffered scientific evidence was wanting and that there were key methodological flaws in the evidence that warranted its exclusion. Accordingly, the court excluded each of the experts' opinions, leading ultimately to the termination of the litigation because the plaintiffs lacked any reliable scientific evidence demonstrating that the Mirena IUD was capable of causing the various alleged injuries.

Not only does the *Mirena* litigation provide a further illustration of a court expeditiously dispensing with large-scale multidistrict litigation through motion practice on common issues, it also shows that the resolution of such issues is not necessarily a one-way street. The plaintiffs in the *Mirena* litigation also moved to exclude the opinions offered by the defense witnesses in the litigation. However, in assessing the scientific evidence, the court rejected the plaintiffs' contentions, finding that the defense experts' opinions were supported by reliable scientific evidence.[108]

While plaintiffs do not routinely raise such common issues in multidistrict litigation, it may be that in the future plaintiffs will raise such issues more frequently at the pre-trial stage. After all, the procedural rules are neutral in nature and apply equally to both sides in a civil dispute. Plaintiffs may find it to their advantage to raise common issues in MDL proceedings to obtain rulings on key issues that may make it more likely defendants will engage in settlement negotiations to resolve the litigation.

Rulings on causation in MDL proceedings may also end up narrowing the scope of the litigation rather than entirely eliminating it. This occurred in multidistrict litigation alleging that the medication phenylpropanolamine (PPA), a common decongestant found in over-the-counter cough and cold medications, was associated with strokes and other conditions. There, the defendants maintained that there was no reliable scientific evidence linking PPA with stroke more than 72 hours after administration of the drug. In other words, any reaction that could be associated with stroke occurred relatively promptly after administration. The defendants further argued that the only possible injury with which PPA was associated was stroke. It was not associated with any of the myriad other injuries plaintiffs in the MDL had cited.

The district court presiding over the MDL agreed and granted the defendants' *Daubert* motions seeking to exclude plaintiffs' causation evidence. In doing so, the court significantly narrowed the scope of the litigation by eliminating a number of alleged injuries and placing a temporal requirement on any alleged injury due to stroke.[109] Accordingly, the *PPA* ruling illustrates how dispositive motion practice may address common issues that can significantly narrow the litigation.

Judge Barbara Rothstein, who presided over the MDL, later wrote a law review article describing the litigation. As Judge Rothstein observed, such narrowing of the proceedings through *Daubert* motions challenging the reliability of the scientific evidence supporting the claims is "a major vehicle for reducing meritless claims in a large litigation": "The approach employed in *In re PPA* has become accepted as a model case management technique for incorporating the trends toward global resolution of scientific issues while respecting the limitations placed on the transferee judge by the *Lexecon* decision."[110] Indeed, as noted, courts have since issued a series of rulings excluding scientific evidence under *Daubert* that have eliminated all, or large categories of, claims in MDL proceedings involving a variety of personal injury or product liability cases. In fact, as the examples described herein illustrate, such rulings appear to be more common in recent years.

Other Common Issues

Generic motion practice may focus on issues that are more legal in nature than the scientific issues that arose in the *PPA, Mirena*, and *Lipitor* MDLs. The litigation alleging that the osteoporosis medication Fosamax caused bone fractures provides an example. The defendants argued that federal law preempted the claims because the FDA essentially had rejected stronger warnings regarding bone fractures. Relying on Supreme Court precedent, the defendants argued that, based on the record before the agency, there was clear evidence the FDA would have rejected warnings the plaintiffs maintained should have been given.[111]

The trial court agreed and granted defendants summary judgment, concluding that a reasonable jury could not have ruled in favor of plaintiffs because the issue of bone fractures was raised with the FDA, and the FDA did not require stronger warnings. However, when the plaintiffs appealed this ruling, the appellate court reversed, concluding that the factual record was not clear enough to grant summary judgment. The appellate court rejected the defendants' contention that the preemption issue should be reserved to judges alone. It concluded that the question turned on disputed issues of fact that should be decided by a jury, much like any other factual question.

The Supreme Court, however, agreed with the defendants that the preemption issue was one that was legal in nature and should be decided by judges, rather than juries. The Court reasoned that the clear evidence standard it had articulated previously was not an evidentiary standard and that judges were in the best position to decide questions based largely on an administrative record before the FDA. Accordingly, the Court remanded the case so the lower court could reevaluate the preemption ruling consistent with the Supreme Court's opinion.

Manufacturers have successfully invoked the preemption defense in other MDLs. For example, there have been several MDLs in which generic pharmaceutical manufacturers have prevailed in arguing that the claims against them were preempted by federal law. These manufacturers have pointed to the fact that they are required by federal law to label their products in the same fashion as the brand name version of the product. Accordingly, they lack control over the labeling pursuant to federal statutory law and cannot add additional warnings that plaintiffs may maintain are warranted. As the Supreme Court held in *PLIVA, Inc. v. Mensing*, "when a party cannot satisfy its state duties without the Federal Government's special permission and assistance, which is dependent on the exercise of judgment by a federal agency, that party cannot independently satisfy those state duties for pre-emption purposes."[112]

Another issue courts have confronted in MDL proceedings that is primarily legal in nature is the adequacy of warnings accompanying a product. Pharmaceutical product liability claims typically are based on allegations that the manufacturer failed to warn of certain risks associated with the product. Accordingly, courts in MDLs involving product liability cases may be called upon to determine whether the language contained in warning labels adequately discloses the risks that plaintiffs allege.

The *Meridia* MDL provides an example. There, the plaintiffs alleged that a medication used to promote weight loss in obese patients increased blood pressure and heart rate, which, in turn, increased the risk of various adverse cardiovascular events. The defendants pursued a two-pronged argument in their summary judgment motion. First, they argued that there was no evidence the product caused adverse cardiovascular events. At the same time, however, they argued in the alternative that the warning in the labeling was adequate because the label indicated the medication could increase blood pressure and heart rate.

The court focused on the latter ground. The court examined whether the warning was adequate and concluded that it was. The court reasoned that, even though there was nothing specifically warning about cardiovascular adverse events in the label, physicians would know that increases in blood pressure or heart rate could lead to increased risk for such events: "Physicians are well aware of the scope of the risks associated with increased blood pressure and do not need specifics regarding the possible consequences of blood pressure increases."[113] Accordingly, the court granted summary judgment on all claims, effectively terminating the MDL proceeding.

The MDL involving the Norplant contraceptive provides a similar example. That litigation involved allegations that the warnings accompanying the contraceptive were not adequate and failed to disclose side effects such as headaches, mood swings, depression, nausea, and other miscellaneous ailments. The defendants maintained that the warnings were adequate to inform plaintiffs' physicians of the alleged risks associated with the product. The court agreed, finding that claims relating to 26 conditions contained in the labeling were barred because the warnings were adequate to disclose the risks.[114]

This ruling, however, was combined with another ruling that effectively terminated the litigation. In addition to the 26 conditions disclosed in the labeling, various plaintiffs in the litigation also raised a number of disparate conditions not contained in the labeling. The court dispensed with those claims on the ground that there was no science establishing that Norplant caused the conditions.[115]

Other legal issues may similarly bar claims filed in a product liability MDL. In the *TMJ Implants Products Liability* litigation, for example, plaintiffs alleged that silicone implants caused various diseases. They sued the supplier of the silicone used by another company to manufacture the implants. The court granted summary judgment in favor of the suppliers of the silicone, citing the principle that "suppliers of inherently safe 'component parts are not responsible for accidents that result when the parts are integrated into a larger system that the component part supplier did not design or build.'"[116]

As these examples illustrate, there can be a variety of issues that lend themselves to generic motion practice. These may include whether there is a product defect, whether warnings are adequate, whether the product causes the alleged injuries, whether the claims are preempted, whether the statute of limitations has run, whether particular states' laws support a cause of action, and many other issues. The resolution of such omnibus issues is a common method for resolving claims or narrowing the scope of the litigation in many MDL proceedings. Indeed, it is precisely such generic motion practice that the MDL statute seemed to contemplate when it provided for consolidated pre-trial proceedings with respect to claims that share common issues.

6
Resolving Individual Cases and Case-Specific Issues

While the MDL process can achieve significant efficiencies by resolving issues common among claims, that does not mean the process does not also add efficiency in resolving case-specific issues. Centralization of the litigation before a single judge results in greater efficiency in the resolution of case-specific issues because, while the issues may vary in each case, there will still be some degree of overlap among cases. As the court becomes more familiar with the types of issues that arise in individual cases, it can more effectively resolve such issues as they arise. Likewise, the parties receive guidance as the court addresses individual motions, which should facilitate the consensual resolution of issues in other cases.

In addition, there is not necessarily a bright-line division between generic and case-specific issues. While some case-specific issues may be unique to individual cases, others may relate to a cluster of cases. For example, whether a plaintiff's claim is barred by the statute of limitations may involve issues that are somewhat common to multiple claims, as well as individualized issues. The knowledge of a particular plaintiff would be unique to that plaintiff. However, there may be a general rule that is common among the claims regarding when a claim accrues or when the time for filing a claim starts to run under the statute of limitations. Likewise, there may be a common issue regarding when plaintiffs should have known of their claim based on publicly available information. Thus, case-specific issues may be intermingled with those that are more generic.

However, case-specific issues have not always received the attention they deserve in large MDL proceedings. Perhaps because some judges have viewed resolution of case-specific issues as being more time consuming, less attention has been given to such issues in MDL proceedings. As critics of the MDL system have observed, "because multidistrict proceedings by design have tended to prioritize global issues over individual ones, plaintiffs' counsel have successfully warehoused meritless claims and shielded them from judicial scrutiny in a way they never could if all cases were being tried individually."[117] Accordingly, to effectively resolve an MDL, it is critical that not only the common issues raised by the claims be given significant attention, but also that these case-specific issues, which may be dispositive of large numbers of claims in the litigation, be addressed and resolved by the MDL court.

Motion Practice in Individual Cases

One obvious way of addressing case-specific issues is through motion practice in individual cases. However, there are other mechanisms courts have used successfully to resolve individualized issues in MDL cases. Courts have employed show cause orders, *Lone Pine* or similar orders, voluntary dismissals, the threat of sanctions, and other mechanisms to help facilitate the elimination of claims that lack merit based on case-specific determinations. Each of these mechanisms has proved successful in eliminating claims that lack merit.

Such mechanisms can function in parallel with generic motion practice with respect to common issues and, indeed, some of the most successful MDLs have involved multiple approaches in scrutinizing asserted claims. One example is the litigation over the anticoagulant heparin. The *Heparin* MDL involved allegations that an anticoagulant was contaminated with impurities that caused a variety of adverse events, including patient deaths. Most of the claims in the MDL were resolved through two separate tracks.

The first track involved certain issues that were common among the claims. This included whether claims involving alleged injuries occurring more than 60 minutes after administration were supported by scientific evidence. It also included whether claims that involved subcutaneous administration rather than intravenous administration were supported by the scientific evidence. The court concluded that these claims lacked reliable scientific evidence and granted summary judgment on the ground that they were speculative.[118] Published research indicated that, to the extent patients experienced adverse events, they occurred within the first 60 minutes after administration. Research also found that the adverse events only occurred where patients were administered the heparin intravenously; subcutaneous administration was not sufficient to cause any adverse event. After ruling on these generic issues, it was then merely an administrative matter to determine which claims fell within these buckets.

At the same time, the court pursued a second, independent track that involved case-specific issues. Specifically, there were issues regarding what might be characterized as product identification in the individual cases. Not all of the claims involved individuals who received contaminated heparin. In some cases, there was proof the plaintiffs had not received contamination at all. In other cases, given the timing of the alleged injury, it was extremely unlikely the patient had received a contaminated dose of heparin.

In resolving these cases, defense counsel went through the records and sought to have plaintiff counsel voluntarily dismiss those cases in which exposure to contamination was unlikely. In some cases, this voluntary approach was successful, and where it worked, it eliminated the need to burden the MDL court with the issue. However, in other cases, plaintiff counsel refused to voluntarily dismiss the cases and, in such circumstances, the defendants filed motions for summary judgment.

The court promptly ruled on these motions filed in the individual cases and, as the court did so, it provided further guidance to the parties. As a result, the ability to come to a consensual resolution regarding exposure became easier when it was clear to plaintiff counsel that the court was more than willing to consider and rule on motions in the individual cases. As a result, there was an incentive for plaintiffs to screen their cases and voluntarily dismiss those in which there was inadequate evidence of exposure to contamination, given that there was potential damage to the reputation of the lawyers who continuously sought to pursue meritless cases in the face of dispositive motions.

Another example in which an MDL court utilized motion practice to resolve individual claims occurred in the *Silica* MDL. As in the *Heparin* litigation, however, in some respects the procedures employed were a hybrid approach in that there was by happenstance an element of commonality in the issues before the court. The *Silica* litigation involved allegations that silica dust was associated with silicosis, a disease of the lungs. The litigation was similar to prior asbestos litigation in that the claims frequently were diagnosed through mass screenings by a handful of physicians paid by plaintiff counsel. As a result, thousands of claims were filed in the MDL alleging that silica caused lung disease, a significant number compared to what one might expect in the general population. In total, "over 9,000 Plaintiffs who submitted Fact Sheets were diagnosed with silicosis by only 12 doctors."[119] Accordingly, while each plaintiff received an individual diagnosis, the methodology employed in diagnosing the plaintiffs was common to some extent in that there were a small number of physicians who actually performed these diagnoses.

The court utilized a *Daubert* proceeding to investigate the reliability of the plaintiff diagnoses. After scrutinizing the claims, the court concluded that the "'epidemic' of some 10,000 cases of silicosis 'is largely the result of misdiagnosis.'"[120] After examining their opinions and receiving testimony from the handful of physicians who provided these diagnoses, the court concluded that the doctors "utilized shockingly relaxed standards of diagnosing that they would never have employed on themselves, their families or their patients in their clinical practices."[121] Indeed, the court concluded that the methodology the doctors used was so egregiously flawed that the claims that were filed were "driven by neither health nor justice: they were manufactured for money."[122]

The *Silica* litigation provides an example of what can go wrong with plaintiff recruitment in a large MDL proceeding. Not only were the procedures used to support the claims dramatically flawed, but as later commentators noted, the plaintiffs appeared to have been drawn from prior mass tort cases: "[A]fter the threatened demise of asbestos litigation triggered a rush to file silicosis claims, thousands of asbestos plaintiffs were 'recycled' as silicosis plaintiffs."[123]

Issues regarding the reliability of medical diagnoses are not the only basis on which individual claims may be eliminated. As in the *Heparin* litigation, issues regarding whether the plaintiffs were actually exposed to a defective product may lead to the elimination of individual claims. In the *Digitek* MDL, for example, the court found that the litigation was premised on a wholesale filing of claims in which the plaintiffs could not establish exposure to a defective product. The plaintiffs in the *Digitek* MDL alleged that certain tablets of a drug manufactured by the defendant were defective because they were larger than they were supposed to be and contained an increased dose of the medication. However, none of the plaintiffs in the litigation were able to prove the defendant had actually sold lots of the drug that contained the alleged defect: "not a single double-thick Digitek was ever found outside the plant."[124] While *Digitek* is a somewhat unusual case, it is *not* unusual for there to be cases filed in MDLs in which individual plaintiffs were not exposed to a defective product or, indeed, were not even exposed to the type of product at issue in the litigation. Such claims are relatively common in large MDLs involving product liability claims.

Procedures similar to those employed in these examples have been used in other MDL proceedings to address a variety of case-specific issues. In addition to the validity of plaintiff diagnoses, exposure to a defective product, and the reliability of the scientific evidence supporting causation in individual cases, courts have addressed a variety of other issues, such as whether the statute of limitations has expired or whether the elements of the claims are satisfied under specific states' laws in individual cases.

Moreover, while many of these examples have involved motions for summary judgment or *Daubert* motions, many commentators have advocated that MDL courts apply increased scrutiny of asserted claims at the pleading stage as well. According to some critics,[125] there is a widespread failure to properly plead claims filed in MDL proceedings, and many of the cases filed do not satisfy the pleading requirements under *Ashcroft v. Iqbal*[126] and *Bell Atlantic Corp. v. Twombly.*[127] Such scrutiny may weed out claims brought by plaintiffs who are not able to plead basic facts such as exposure and injury consistent with their obligations under Rule 11 of the Federal Rules of Civil Procedure. However, in other cases, a motion to dismiss may not be dispositive of the litigation; the court may simply give plaintiffs leave to replead to add allegations to their complaint necessary to sustain their claims.

In addition to meeting the pleading requirements under *Twombly* and *Iqbal*, however, there are other significant issues that courts may decide warrant dismissal as a matter of law at the pleading stage. For example, many states have particularly stringent state tort law requirements. Plaintiffs whose claims are governed by these states' laws may find themselves legally barred from bringing a claim, whereas plaintiffs in other states may be able to proceed with similar claims due to differences in the law among the various states. Similarly, some plaintiffs' complaints may show on their face that their claims are time-barred. They may plead a date of injury that shows they filed their claims after the statute of limitations had expired. Accordingly, it is not unusual for MDL courts to determine that individual cases or groups of cases are barred at the motion to dismiss stage.

To facilitate review at the pleading stage, however, it may be necessary for the court to put in place procedures that ensure each plaintiff actually provides an initial pleading that is adequate for review. For example, while most plaintiffs in large MDLs file individual complaints, occasionally plaintiff counsel seek to lump multiple plaintiffs into a single complaint. When this occurs, it may be difficult to determine whether each plaintiff has adequately pleaded a claim. In addition, the court is deprived of revenue from filing fees plaintiffs must pay each time a new complaint is filed.

Where plaintiffs have filed such consolidated complaints, MDL courts have taken actions to require that plaintiffs are severed and file individual complaints that adequately plead each individual's claim. Not only does this ensure the courts will have an initial pleading to review, but as MDL courts have observed, the filing fee to some extent plays a gatekeeping role itself by providing a monetary disincentive to filing frivolous claims.[128] Where the fee requirement is enforced, it ensures plaintiff counsel at least has sufficient confidence in the individual claim that he or she is willing to pay the filing fee to bring the case to court.

In the *Taxotere (Docetaxel) Products Liability* litigation, for example, the court issued an order severing multi-party cases. Within a specific number of days following transfer to the MDL proceeding, the court required the plaintiffs to request severance of their claims, and then within a certain number of days following a severance order, the individual plaintiffs were required to file complaints and pay the filing fees.[129] The court thereby prevented plaintiffs from evading the filing fee that would be required if they each filed an individual complaint and also potentially facilitated review of the individual claims at the pleading stage.

Despite such orders, in large product liability MDL proceedings there are some trends that may hamper the use of motions to dismiss to narrow the litigation. Many MDL courts allow plaintiffs to file short-form complaints that may not contain all of the information necessary to assess whether the claims should be dismissed. Such short-form complaints are frequently allowed in MDLs where the court directs that plaintiffs file a master complaint that is general in nature and covers all of the asserted claims. While such procedures may save plaintiffs time and effort, they are somewhat inconsistent with the Federal Rules of Civil Procedure, which require each plaintiff to file a complaint that adequately pleads a claim for relief. Moreover, unless each plaintiff is required to plead specifics supporting their claims, there may not be a basis for dismissing the claim on the pleadings.

There are, however, other types of MDLs where motions to dismiss can be very significant. MDLs that involve antitrust claims may be resolved entirely, or at least significantly narrowed, based on motions to dismiss. Indeed, the *Twombly* case itself involved a motion to dismiss antitrust claims. Frequently, in antitrust cases such motions can be dispositive if, for example, the plaintiff cannot plead sufficient detail to establish that there was a conspiracy to fix prices. Accordingly, different types of dispositive motions may be more or less significant in an MDL proceeding, depending on the nature of the substantive claims in the litigation.

Other Mechanisms for Resolving Case-Specific Issues

Motion practice is not the only mechanism courts have employed to eliminate claims based on their individual defects. Rather, courts have used a variety of administrative orders and more informal means to work through the asserted claims. In some instances, these orders impose requirements on plaintiffs they cannot, or are unwilling to, meet. In some instances, the court provides incentives for plaintiffs to take voluntary action to dismiss their claims. Using such mechanisms, courts have eliminated many claims while expending little in the way of judicial time or resources. Such orders essentially shift the burden onto the plaintiffs themselves to screen their cases thoroughly. In doing so, they move toward restoring the normal balance, requiring plaintiffs to adequately investigate their claims before filing them.

In the *Welding Fume* MDL, for example, the court utilized a case-management order to encourage plaintiffs to eliminate claims that had no merit. The *Welding Fume* MDL involved thousands of claims alleging that manganese in fumes from welding rods was associated with the development of Parkinson's disease in welders. The court did not begin the MDL proceeding by putting in place measures to weed out meritless claims. However, after years of litigation, the court began to recognize that such measures were necessary to make progress in the proceeding.[130]

As with many MDLs, the court learned that many of the cases filed in the MDL lacked merit during the course of the bellwether selection process. The court discovered there were problems with the cases that had been selected as test cases when plaintiffs started to voluntarily dismiss the cases rather than trying them. Indeed, some of the cases appeared to involve outright fraud, as individuals who claimed to be injured had been videotaped engaging in vigorous physical activity. After investigating further, the court learned that the vast majority of the plaintiffs who had filed claims in the MDL had been diagnosed by the same handful of doctors who conducted mass screenings of prospective plaintiffs, raising the possibility that these doctors were not reliably diagnosing Parkinson's disease in a significant number of the cases: "Almost all the plaintiffs in the litigation were diagnosed at mass medico-legal screenings, in which plaintiff-hired neurologists conducted five-minute examinations and then diagnosed thousands of welders with this rare disorder."[131] Such mass screenings led the doctors to offer opinions that plaintiffs had Parkinson's disease, when they did not.

Having made these observations, the court put in place procedures to require plaintiffs to submit a diagnosis by an independent physician establishing that each plaintiff actually had Parkinson's disease and that, in the physician's opinion, the disease was caused by fumes from welding rods.[132] This simple administrative procedure resulted in the elimination of numerous claims. Many plaintiffs were unwilling or unable to come up with the required diagnoses and simply dropped their lawsuits. Nonetheless, the defendants were forced to litigate these baseless claims for years, illustrating the significant inefficiencies caused by MDL proceedings that are clogged with meritless cases and underscoring that such measures should have been taken much earlier in the proceedings.

This process of culling claims by administrative order did not end the litigation but did significantly narrow its scope. Perhaps indicative of the quality of the remaining claims (or lack thereof), most of the trials that occurred resulted in verdicts in favor of the defendants.[133] Thus, while the court ultimately ended up successfully addressing one aspect of the claims in question by issuing a simple case-management order, there may have been other issues regarding the validity of the claims that remained unresolved by this procedure. While the case-management order addressed the issue of unreliable diagnoses, it did not address other elements of plaintiffs' claims that may also have been problematic.

The order entered in the *Welding Fume* litigation is similar to so-called *Lone Pine* orders that have been utilized in other MDL proceedings, requiring an affidavit from an independent physician to support the asserted claims. In fact, the Duke guidelines recommend such orders as a best practice, particularly where causation is disputed or where there are multiple potential causes of an alleged injury: "These orders are particularly important in an MDL proceeding involving disparate theories of causation—or when multiple alternative potential causes of the alleged injuries exist."[134]

From a defense perspective, one potential downside of requesting such a procedure may be that it requires plaintiffs to support their claims where they otherwise might not do so. Depending on the circumstances, for defendants it may make more sense to file a motion seeking summary judgment on the claims rather than going through the extra step of having plaintiffs produce additional substantiation, which, in turn, might allow plaintiffs to avoid dismissal. Accordingly, depending on the facts and circumstances of the particular case, there may be strategic considerations that weigh in favor of, or against, adopting such procedures.

In practice, where such procedures are implemented, plaintiffs in MDL proceedings generally have been unable or unwilling to come up with an affidavit from an independent expert to support their claims. And even if they supply some form of documentation in response to such a court order, it may not be substantiated or reliable, providing additional grounds for attacking the claim. Accordingly, administrative orders along the lines of that issued by the court in the *Welding Fumes* MDL can be an effective mechanism for examining the validity of pending cases and eliminating those that should not proceed. In sum, there are many claims filed in MDLs that will fall by the wayside if the court adopts measures that require plaintiffs to take even minimal steps to prosecute the claims. Either because the claims are inherently flawed or because their value is not worth the effort to comply with such orders, a number of plaintiffs simply drop their claims when required to take some of the steps they would ordinarily have to take if they were pursuing their lawsuits as individual cases filed outside of an MDL proceeding.

Another means of addressing case-specific issues was utilized to good effect in the massive MDL involving asbestos personal injury claims. The *Asbestos* MDL had been lingering in the federal courts for years, handling thousands of asbestos personal injury claims that had been filed in, or removed to, federal court. When Judge Eduardo Robreno was designated to take over the proceedings, he therefore had a daunting task. The cases were not ones that necessarily lent themselves to generic motion practice. The parties were not disputing, for example, whether asbestos was capable of causing injuries in at least some individuals. Rather, most of the disputes centered around case-specific issues, such as whether asbestos had caused a particular plaintiff's disease (specific causation) or whether the plaintiff was exposed to a particular defendant's product. Thus, resolving the claims in the asbestos MDL would require significant effort to scrutinize the facts and circumstances of each individual claim.

Upon his appointment, Judge Robreno set up procedures for the orderly resolution of thousands of claims pending in the MDL. The court utilized magistrates to assist in the review of case-specific issues in the individual cases, such as causation and exposure. This review was coupled with motion practice on the individual claims where necessary. Instead of merely requiring an affidavit from an independent physician, as in the *Welding Fume* MDL, the court's requirements were more stringent and resembled more closely the normal process of litigating individual cases in the federal system. The court established a schedule for each case similar to the scheduling orders one might see in an individual case that required, among other things, plaintiffs to submit reports from independent experts based on "medically accepted principles and practices" as well as a complete history of the plaintiff's exposure to asbestos, followed by dispositive motion practice.[135]

Utilizing these procedures, the court was able to resolve approximately 200,000 claims and eventually close out the asbestos MDL proceeding.[136] Thus, this case provides a striking example of how an MDL court was able to litigate thousands of individual claims effectively without relying on a global settlement for resolution. In doing so, the court found that many of the claims suffered from common problems. As in the *Welding Fume* and *Silica* litigation, there were frequently problems with the diagnoses of the individual plaintiffs provided by their medical experts. Judge Robreno reported that "[t]he rate of 'positive' findings by these doctors can be startlingly high, often upwards of 50% and in some studies as high as 90%, suggesting that the readings may not be neutral or legitimate."[137]

In some ways, this was not news. There had been much written regarding the problem of meritless claims in asbestos litigation. Justice Breyer, for example, had famously observed that, "up to one-half of asbestos claims are now being filed by people who have little or no physical impairment. Many of these claims produce substantial payments (and substantial costs) even though individual litigants will never become impaired."[138] The problem Judge Robreno faced was distinguishing between the claims that lacked merit and those that should receive compensation.

However, using the procedures the court had put in place, which largely mirrored the normal rules of civil procedure, these sorts of problems were easily uncovered. The asbestos MDL therefore illustrates that, even in the largest MDLs, it is possible to provide thorough review for individual claims to ensure that only meritorious claims are eligible for compensation. The court adjudicated thousands of disputed claims utilizing time-tested procedures for addressing claims under the federal rules, demonstrating that there is no need to abandon the normal procedures in an MDL proceeding in the interest of expediency.

MDL courts have used more aggressive procedures for encouraging the elimination of meritless claims where the circumstances warranted. While federal courts are often hesitant to impose sanctions on the parties or their lawyers, MDL courts have issued sanctions orders to get a handle on cases in which plaintiffs are filing claims that are essentially frivolous. In the *Mentor Obtape Transobturator Sling* MDL, for example, the court issued an order indicating it would consider imposing sanctions in cases where plaintiffs had filed claims that did not survive summary judgment. The MDL involved allegations that a surgical mesh product caused various injuries to women. As it ruled on motions for summary judgment in the individual cases, the court found that there were many cases in which the plaintiffs failed to support their claims of causation or where they continued to file claims that were time-barred. Accordingly, the court entered an order stating that counsel would be sanctioned if they did not withdraw cases that lacked merit.

The procedural mechanism the court selected to implement this ruling was to issue show-cause orders as to why sanctions should not be imposed that would accompany summary judgment rulings in the cases where "no good faith basis existed for maintaining the action through the summary judgment stage."[139] The court implemented this procedural mechanism for encouraging plaintiff counsel to better screen their cases based on its experience in ruling on motions for summary judgment in the individual cases.

The court suggested the number of claims in the MDL had "exploded" at least "in part" due to "an onslaught of lawyer television solicitations." However, plaintiff counsel were failing to screen these new cases and instead were filing claims they "should have known" lacked "any good faith basis." As the court observed, as a result of the lack of adequate screening and prosecution of the cases filed in the MDL, the court "had to waste judicial resources deciding motions in cases that should have been dismissed by plaintiff's counsel earlier—cases that probably should never have been brought in the first place."[140] Accordingly, the court ruled that, "in future orders granting summary judgment in which no good faith basis existed for maintaining the action through the summary judgment stage, the Court intends to include an addendum in the order requiring counsel to show cause why sanctions should not be imposed."[141]

Raising the specter of sanctions, as the court did in the *Mentor* litigation, certainly provides a financial incentive for plaintiff firms to better screen their cases. If courts in MDL proceedings began to assess financial penalties on law firms that file claims that are obviously meritless, the practice would likely decline in prevalence. Currently, there is little in the way of financial disincentive to filing such claims. Plaintiff law firms do incur some costs for each claim filed. In addition to filing fees and administrative costs of keeping track of the claims, there are typically costs associated with pursuing the claims, such as the time and cost associated with completing fact sheets and responding to discovery. However, these costs are much lower than they would be if the cases were filed as individual claims. Accordingly, the potential imposition of sanctions would be a significant disincentive to filing frivolous claims.

As some of these examples illustrate, many MDL courts have failed to address the problem of meritless claims until late in the proceedings. Either because they do not realize the scope of the problem, or because of inertia, or perhaps a hope that the claims will settle, there are a number of instances in which courts end up addressing meritless claims only toward the end of the proceedings. As the authorities recognize, however, this is far from ideal. Courts should attempt to put in place meaningful procedures to clear out unsupported claims at the outset of an MDL proceeding.

This is not only a more efficient means of addressing claims in an MDL proceeding, but it is a task that inevitably must be performed in some fashion even where the result of an MDL proceeding is settlement. Just as the parties must determine which claims will receive compensation if they are litigated in the tort system, so, too, a decision must be made concerning the proper allocation of funds when there is a settlement. Simply providing all plaintiffs the same compensation regardless of the merit of their claims is inherently problematic.

Accordingly, even where there is a settlement, typically there is some mechanism for attempting to assess the merits of asserted claims and to adjust compensation accordingly.

As noted previously, the *Propulsid* litigation provides a frequently cited example that illustrates how settlement funds may be allocated and the potential pitfalls of failing to eliminate meritless claims early in the proceedings. It demonstrates that where claims are not eliminated on the front end, the problems with the claims frequently must be addressed on the back end. The result is that no efficiency is achieved by rushing toward settlement. In addition, unintended and inequitable results may occur.

Thus, as previously discussed, in the *Propulsid* MDL, plaintiff counsel received a windfall, recovering millions of dollars when only a few of the plaintiffs were eligible for recovery.[142] This inequitable outcome occurred because there was a mismatch between the inventory considered for purposes of the calculation of fees and the inventory that ultimately received compensation. The fees were based on an assumption that most claims in the MDL were viable and that plaintiff counsel should receive compensation based on their obtaining a significant recovery for most of their clients, whereas in reality most of the claims ended up not being eligible for compensation when the settlement criteria were applied to them. As a consequence, plaintiff counsel received a large recovery while most of their clients received nothing.

Similarly, in the *Vioxx* MDL—which involved one of the larger MDL settlements—very few of the claims ultimately met even the non-rigorous criteria for recovery that were put in place under the settlement agreement. While a number of claims in the *Vioxx* litigation went to trial, scrutiny of the larger universe of claims did not really occur until the settlement stage. As a result, as in *Propulsid*, comparatively few claims received compensation.[143] Indeed, while data regarding the allocation of settlement funds are not readily available for most MDLs, those involved in the process have reported that it is common for only 30 to 40 percent of the asserted claims to receive compensation.[144] Thus, there is a significant problem that does not get the recognition it deserves simply because of a lack of transparency in MDL proceedings.

Another option for termination of an MDL proceeding other than settlement or litigation before the MDL court is to remand the cases back to the federal courts from which they were transferred. In the past, MDL courts have attempted to avoid this outcome. However, the Federal Judicial Center recently suggested that federal MDL judges consider it as an option: "When you have completed all common discovery, ruled on all pretrial motions, and exhausted reasonable settlement attempts, it may be time to recommend that the Panel remand those unresolved cases to their transferor districts.... Do not hesitate to take this action (or to suggest that you might take it) when coordinated or consolidated pretrial proceedings no longer serve a valid purpose."[145] Indeed, the MDL statute specifically contemplates that after pre-trial proceedings are completed, the cases will be remanded to the transferor courts.[146]

Moreover, it is not uncommon for MDL courts to remand small numbers of claims where the court has largely completed its work. As defendants become more resistant to resolving claims in an MDL and more resistant to settlement, remands may become more likely: "Increasingly judges and counsel are not only recognizing that remand is a viable option when pretrial matters are complete and no resolution has been reached, but that it may be on the table from the first days of the MDL. . . ."[147]

As with settlement, there is a recognition that terminating an MDL proceeding through remand does not eliminate the need to go through and weed out meritless claims. As commentators recognize, the best approach is to eliminate claims early in a proceeding, but to the extent that has not been done, such scrutiny should be provided before claims are sent back to the transferor courts. Indeed, the Duke guidelines specifically recommend that the MDL court cull cases before remand because it is in the best position to do so: "In preparation for remand, the court should consider using *Lone Pine* proceedings or other methods to cull meritless cases and ensure that only the viable cases may ultimately be eligible for remand."[148] Having presided over the litigation, typically for a period of years, the MDL court is more familiar with the cases than the transferor courts and can better assess the merits of the claims and make other pre-trial rulings. The guidelines seek to maximize the work of the MDL court in that respect and thus maximize the efficiency of MDL proceedings before the cases are sent back to the transferor courts for final resolution.

Accordingly, even where the outcome of an MDL proceeding is remand of the remaining cases to the courts that originally had them, it is incumbent on the MDL court to undertake the effort to go through the claims and assess them to determine whether they are viable. If the MDL court fails to do so, it will be up to the individual federal courts that receive the cases to educate themselves regarding the merits and assess the merits themselves—resulting in a much more inefficient and expensive process than resolution in the context of a centralized MDL proceeding.

7
The Bellwether Process

While pre-trial assessment of the viability of a claim is a task the MDL statute seems to contemplate specifically, MDL courts have, as a matter of practice, undertaken other roles that do not seem to fall as squarely within their jurisdiction—if they fall within their jurisdiction at all. One of the primary functions MDL courts have performed that falls in this category is presiding over trials of test cases, or bellwethers. The motivation behind this practice is to give the parties some idea of the value and viability of the claims in order to facilitate settlement. Not only may the parties gain basic information regarding how frequently juries will award verdicts in favor of plaintiffs and the amounts of such verdicts, but they also may obtain more detailed information regarding the theories that work and do not work at trial, the importance of central pieces of evidence, and the credibility of fact and expert witnesses.

The goal therefore is not to resolve every case through trial in the MDL proceeding, but rather to obtain representative results that may inform the parties in attempting to reach a settlement: "The more representative the bellwether cases, the more reliable the information about similar cases will be."[149] As the Federal Judicial Center has noted, "[t]hese test cases should produce a sufficient number of representative verdicts and settlements to enable the parties and the court to determine the nature and strength of the claims, whether they can be fairly developed and litigated on a group basis, and what range of values the cases may have if resolution is attempted on a group basis."[150]

If the test cases are not representative of the wider universe of claims or the bellwether selection process is flawed in some way, then the entire process may be largely a waste of time. As one MDL judge has noted, "[i]deally, the trial-selection process should accurately reflect the individual categories of cases that comprise the MDL *in toto*, illustrate the likelihood of success and measure of damages within each respective category, and illuminate the forensic and practical challenges of presenting certain types of cases to a jury. Any trial-selection process that strays from this path will likely resolve only a few independent cases and have a limited global impact."[151] Thus, if the parties and the court are going to undertake a bellwether trial process, the process for selecting cases should be given careful consideration.

As commentators have observed, however, there may be other ends that can be achieved through the bellwether process in the event the parties fail to reach a consensual resolution of the litigation. This may include the generation of materials that can be used in subsequent trials. As Judge Fallon has noted, "[a]t a minimum, the bellwether process should lead to the creation of 'trial packages' that can be utilized by local counsel upon the dissolution of MDLs."[152] The very process of preparing for trial creates a significant amount of work product, such as witness outlines, sets of key exhibits, and filings for the court on various evidentiary and other issues. Accordingly, even if no settlement is reached, the bellwether process is not necessarily a wasted effort. Cases must be tried, and the bellwether process may help the parties prepare for those trials in the event the parties cannot immediately reach a settlement of the litigation.

Moreover, as noted in previous chapters, the bellwether process often gives the MDL court insight into the nature of the claims that can be helpful in resolving the remaining cases on a pre-trial basis through motion practice or some other procedural mechanism. Frequently, neither the judge nor the parties will have a full understanding of all the intricacies relating to the cases until they go through the process of preparing an actual case for trial. That process can expose significant flaws in the plaintiffs' claims that may be helpful in the resolution of dispositive motions in other cases without the need for trial.

Criticisms of the Bellwether Process

The selection procedures for picking bellwether cases and increasingly whether, and the extent to which, bellwether trials should be held at all are often contentious issues in MDL proceedings. Defendants have become increasingly skeptical of bellwether trials given the track record in prior MDL proceedings, which has been criticized as leading to many arbitrary and inequitable results.[153] Frequently, MDL proceedings seem to degenerate into a race to trial by plaintiffs eager to obtain a large verdict they can leverage to obtain a global settlement.

The selection of bellwethers for trial is frequently flawed. To the extent that representative cases are not picked for trial, the bellwether process loses a good deal of its utility. Trying cases the parties do not believe to be representative provides them with little information on which to base settlement negotiations. Increasingly, defendants view the bellwether selection process in many MDL proceedings as an exercise in gamesmanship where plaintiffs seek to select only their "best" cases for trial to maximize recovery: "There is ... a significant concern that MDL trials are not actually 'representative' of the larger body of cases—and therefore cannot provide a fair estimate of the legitimacy or value of the plaintiffs' claims generally."[154]

Accordingly, defendants have begun to push back on the utilization of bellwether trials in MDL proceedings. As we shall see in a subsequent chapter, the defense bar has proposed reforms that would allow defendants to avoid bellwether trials altogether. However, they have also questioned whether the statutory framework authorizes MDL courts to conduct such trials. As they note, the statute speaks only of consolidation for pre-trial proceedings, and not for trial. The practice of conducting bellwether trials is a judicially created procedure that some argue is outside of the MDL courts' statutory mandate.

As a practical matter, however, it may be difficult to avoid trials before an MDL court completely. While the Supreme Court has held that there are jurisdictional limitations that preclude the MDL court from trying cases originally filed in other jurisdictions without the parties' consent,[155] there is little to prevent the MDL court from seeking to try cases that were originally filed with the MDL court.

Moreover, because it controls when cases are remanded from the MDL proceeding, the MDL court arguably can arrange the schedule such that these trials occur before any remand.

This, of course, results in a non-representative sample of cases that may be selected for trial. The smaller the potential pool of candidates for bellwether selection, the less representative of the overall universe of claims the selection becomes. In *Lexecon v. Milberg Weiss Bershad Hynes & Lerach*, the Supreme Court issued a ruling that potentially limits significantly the pool of cases that may be selected for trial. There, the Court interpreted the statutory framework governing MDL transfer as requiring that cases be tried in the courts where they were originally filed and in which venue would be appropriate: "A district court conducting pretrial proceedings pursuant to § 1407(a) has no authority to invoke § 1404(a) to assign a transferred case to itself for trial."[156] As a result, absent the parties' consent, the MDL court cannot try such transferred cases. Accordingly, where a party insists on exercise of its *Lexecon* rights, the pool of cases available for trial may decrease dramatically. Thus, as a practical matter, the bellwether process can only really function with the consent of the parties. While there may be significant pressure from the court to force compliance with the process, at the end of the day only consensual participation can really result in a useful bellwether process.

This raises a further potential problem with the use of bellwethers. By definition, trials before the MDL court cannot be completely representative. They represent trial in one jurisdiction with a single jury pool. However, in fact, cases from all over the country are typically consolidated in an MDL proceeding. Accordingly, there is diversity in the jurisdictions and circumstances under which cases would be tried absent MDL consolidation. Cases by definition would be tried in multiple jurisdictions before multiple judges and multiple juries, with all the inherent diversity in potential outcomes associated with these factors. Accordingly, the bellwether process that typically occurs before an MDL court is somewhat artificial and non-representative.

One potential measure to mitigate this effect of centralization before a single MDL court would be to remand cases for trial in other jurisdictions: "The transferee judge has authority at any time during centralized proceedings to recommend that the Panel remand a particular case—or even individual claims within a case—to the transferor court.... Such a remand is thus an option even where other centralized proceedings will continue."[157] In fact, commentators have from time to time suggested this remand mechanism as a potential improvement in the bellwether process—at least where the parties view the jurisdiction selected for the MDL proceeding as an outlier. According to supporters of this remand procedure, "[n]ot only would this practice mitigate the risk of a single transferee judge exerting outsized influence on the proceedings, but it also would provide a wider range of information on the strength and weaknesses of individual cases adjudicated by juries and judges in different jurisdictions."[158]

However, the judges who receive these cases would not be as familiar with them as the MDL court would be and would have to get up to speed on cases over which they did not preside during the pre-trial phase of the litigation. They would have to familiarize themselves with the nature of the cases and the MDL court's rulings, which might present some measure of inefficiency and would inevitably take time.

It may be, however, that given the particular facts and circumstances, the balance weighs in favor of conducting trials in the transferor courts and not attempting what would ultimately be a flawed bellwether process in the MDL court. As the Federal Judicial Center has recognized, "[d]epending on the number and representativeness of cases amenable to trial in the transferee court, the best course may be to remand all cases to their transferor courts for trial once all issues appropriate for pretrial consolidation or coordination have been resolved."[159]

Another potential solution would be to request an inter-circuit transfer.[160] This procedure allows the MDL judge to preside over the trial of a remanded case in a different jurisdiction. The procedure requires a showing of necessity and has not been employed frequently. Moreover, at least one court has rejected such a request.[161] Nonetheless, inter-circuit transfer is another option commentators have raised as a possibility for attempting to obtain more representative results.[162] And, it is a procedure that has already been employed in MDL cases such as the *Welding Fume* litigation.[163]

However, whether or not cases are remanded for trial, it may be difficult to obtain representative outcomes. As a practical matter, only a handful of cases are ever tried as bellwethers in any MDL proceeding. Accordingly, there will always be a limit on the representativeness of the cases given the limited number typically tried in conjunction with an MDL proceeding and the large diversity of facts and circumstances that can manifest themselves in the sorts of cases that are part of large MDLs today. As critics continue to observe, "while MDL courts have been trying cases with increased regularity in recent years, it remains unclear whether such a practice is appropriate or promotes the just outcome of the litigation."[164]

Bellwether Selection

Given the importance of at least attempting to obtain a representative sample of cases for bellwether trials, significant focus is typically given to the process for selecting them. A number of different procedures have been proposed or actually utilized in selecting bellwether cases. One potential means of selecting cases is to draw them randomly from the universe of asserted claims. This method has been promoted as a means to obtain a truly representative set of bellwether cases. As a matter of common sense, one would think a totally random selection of cases would lead to a representative sample of cases; indeed, for this reason, this method was suggested several years ago by sources such as the Federal Judicial Center's *Manual for Complex Litigation.*[165]

However, in practice, random selection of cases from the MDL inventory does not always result in random selection of *viable* cases because such cases may be mixed in with a large number of cases that are *not* viable. The fact that random selection is not uniformly employed (at least in its pure form) is another indicator that MDL courts and the participants in MDL proceedings implicitly recognize that cases are not always rigorously screened during the pre-trial stage to determine their validity.

Cases that are legally or factually flawed should not be tried; they should be dismissed or should be the subject of summary judgment. Therefore, if the MDL court has done its job and gone through and scrutinized the universe of claims in the MDL, such cases will not be part of the universe that may be selected as potential bellwethers. However, frequently this is not done and, as a result, when bellwether selection begins, the parties may be selecting from a universe of claims that contain many cases that are not suitable trial candidates.

Even where screening has occurred, however, random selection can result in the trial of bellwether cases that are extremely favorable for the defense or for plaintiffs. Given that relatively few cases are tried in MDL proceedings, if an outlier case is selected randomly, it can have an outsized effect on the outcome. In other words, because the sample size is so small, random selection may not always result in representative cases being selected for trial. Thus, theoretically random selection would be a very good means of selecting cases; however, due to the failures of the MDL system, it is frequently an imperfect means of selection.

In addition, commentators have criticized random selection as "detach[ing] the attorneys from the process."[166] Not only may this lead to some level of dissatisfaction among the parties who might prefer to be involved in the selection process, but it can also undermine the representativeness of cases given that, if cases were tried individually, the lawyers would be the ones selecting which cases to try first. There are strategic considerations in making this decision, and it may be that excluding the lawyers from the selection process undermines the value of the bellwether process to some extent.

Another possibility for selection of bellwether cases is to have the MDL court pick the cases that will be tried as bellwethers in an attempt to identify representative cases. The court could employ a variety of mechanisms in selecting the cases itself. It could pick cases randomly, select cases that it thought were representative based on a review of the facts and circumstances of the cases, select cases falling into certain categories so there will be trials of at least one case from each category, or use some other mechanism.

Such a procedure obviously puts the onus on the court to educate itself about the claims to make an informed decision regarding selection. Other than simply pulling names out of a hat, the court would be required to familiarize itself with the population of claims at least to some extent to perform the selection role. Moreover, this mechanism takes control away from the parties' lawyers and places it with the judge. It therefore injects a potentially large element of uncertainty in the process and places authority with a decision maker who may not be as familiar with the cases that are filed. For this reason, there may be objections to such a procedure by either plaintiffs or defendants who do not want to lose control over the selection process.

The most common means of choosing cases is some version of selection by the parties themselves. Each party may be allotted a certain number of picks from among the population of cases in the MDL. In some MDLs, the parties may have had an opportunity to conduct more extensive discovery on a subset of the MDL population. In other MDLs, the parties may have had an opportunity to conduct wide-ranging discovery in any individual cases in which they wanted to conduct discovery. In either case, if party selection is employed, both sides must utilize the information available to them to research the cases and then make their selections. Party selection thus puts the onus on the parties to ensure the bellwether selection process is successful and imposes costs on the parties not incurred when using procedures such as random selection.

However, allowing the parties to pick the bellwether candidates obviates the concerns with lack of party control over the litigation. In our adversarial system, we put a premium on individual party control of litigation. Active intervention by the courts is less consistent with our traditional system and more akin to a European system of dispute resolution. Allowing the parties to make the selection also ensures that the participants in the process, who theoretically have the most knowledge about the claims and the resources to devote to assessing them, will be making the decisions about which cases are tried.

One potential downside the court must guard against is the potential for gamesmanship by the parties in selecting the bellwether picks such that the bellwethers chosen become less representative. For example, plaintiff counsel may attempt to pick only cases with sympathetic plaintiffs, rock solid causation evidence, and that do not raise other factual or legal issues the defense can use to inject uncertainty into jurors' minds. Defendants may attempt to choose cases where there is some fundamental flaw in the proof that will allow them to obtain a defense verdict. Indeed, the experience in the MDL selection process illustrates that such strategic maneuvers frequently occur during bellwether selection. As noted, MDL judges commonly receive their first education regarding potential problems in the universe of asserted claims when plaintiff counsel voluntarily dismisses cases that were picked for bellwether trials. These voluntary dismissals prevent the trial of weak cases and potential defense verdicts that would illustrate the problems in the universe of asserted claims. In sum, such dismissals frequently provide evidence that there are many cases in the inventory that plaintiff counsel never want to have adjudicated.

Conversely, many plaintiffs view settlement of bellwether cases as a manipulation of the system by defendants. In their view, defendants settle cases that are good for plaintiffs so they will not be tried and bellwether trials will be skewed in defendants' favor. Defendants may counter that the fact of settlement and the settlement amount is a data point that is a useful outcome itself in the bellwether process, given that a settlement provides an estimate of the value of the case, just as if the bellwether were tried and the parties obtained a jury verdict. Indeed, if plaintiffs are correct that defendants are strategically settling cases, settlement values may *overestimate* the value of claims to the extent defendants are paying a premium to avoid bellwether trials they believe would have good outcomes for the plaintiffs.

Moreover, both plaintiffs and defendants may find excuses not to try certain bellwether cases independent of voluntary dismissal or settlement. For example, in his article on the bellwether selection process, Judge Fallon recounts an example where counsel in one of the bellwether cases "withdrew the case from consideration, reporting that his client refused to consent to trial": "Although the attorneys had represented that all of the necessary consents had been obtained, the attorneys apparently never received the client's consent formally, and in light of *Lexecon*, the Vioxx transferee court was precluded from either forcing the selected case to trial or dismissing it for failure to prosecute."[167] Accordingly, there may be a variety of reasons that cases in the bellwether pool do not proceed to trial.

At any rate, participants recognize the process is subject to some degree of manipulation: "Although there may be good-faith reasons for settling or voluntarily dismissing a test case, there are also instances in which the parties do so to manipulate the takeaways from the bellwether process."[168] Accordingly, independent guidelines recommend that, "[t]he transferee judge should adopt rules that will minimize the risk that parties will attempt to 'game' the bellwether trial-selection process to result in test trials of cases that are not representative of the entire case pool."[169]

As noted in prior chapters, one way to mitigate such strategic behavior is to ensure that the universe of asserted claims has received sufficient scrutiny before bellwether selection occurs. To the extent weak cases can be eliminated before bellwethers are chosen, there will be no need for voluntarily dismissals of such cases during the bellwether selection process along with the accompanying inefficiency. Rather, such cases will not be in the universe of cases from which bellwether cases are selected in the first place.

Another way such problems can be avoided is by maximizing the amount of information available to the parties about the claims in the population. To the extent the parties have information about the universe of claims, they can make more accurate decisions regarding which cases are truly representative. It is therefore less likely the parties will pick an outlier case during the selection process. Despite the benefits of obtaining a broad range of information, some courts have cut down to some extent on the information available to the parties by defining a pool of cases that is a subset of the general population of claims from which bellwethers will be selected. That pool, in turn, is then subject to additional discovery. The motivation behind such measures appears to be the view, held by some judges, that individual discovery may be time consuming.[170]

However, in the most efficient MDLs, the parties are continuously working through individual claims and seeking information necessary to eliminate claims that should not have been filed. To the extent a court defines a pool subject to additional inquiry, it is at least implicitly acting inconsistently with this best practice. Nonetheless, in the typical personal injury case, simply obtaining the plaintiff's medical records and analyzing those records goes a long way in assessing the merits of the claims. Likewise, other publicly available sources, such as a plaintiff's social media accounts, may provide additional valuable information that can lead to the dismissal of claims.

Another common mechanism for mitigating potential strategic behavior in the selection of bellwether cases for trial involves providing each side with a certain number of strikes they may exercise to eliminate the other side's bellwether picks. Allowing each side a certain number of strikes ensures that they can remove outlier cases that they believe are not representative from the bellwether pool:

"[B]y permitting each side a certain number of vetoes, you can minimize the chances of an unrepresentative case serving as a bellwether trial."[171] Accordingly, this procedural mechanism tends to result in a more fair and representative selection of cases for bellwether trials.

A related mechanism commentators have suggested as a potential means by which an MDL court might address the problem of non-representativeness is requiring that all parties consent to the trial of any bellwether that is selected. Indeed, some have asserted that, "[t]he best method of selection is to require the attorneys to agree on all cases."[172] This is essentially a stronger version of the strike procedure that gives all parties a veto over any case that results from the bellwether selection process. The theory is that, "[u]nder this approach, outlier cases favoring one side would be unlikely to be selected."[173] Such a mechanism could be utilized not only where the parties pick the bellwether cases, but more generally where bellwethers are selected using a variety of procedures.

However, one could easily envision that there would be difficulty in getting the parties to agree on bellwether cases to be tried. Essentially, the court would be giving all parties a "heckler's veto" that could be used to prevent the trial of any bellwethers a party unilaterally decides it does not want to try, which, in turn, may result in highly unrepresentative cases going to trial. After all, the cases to which *both* sides agree would in practice likely represent a small minority of the cases in any MDL proceeding. One suspects that the vast majority of cases in any population of claims in an MDL proceeding would be cases one party or the other would object to trying.

Finally, in cases where bellwether candidates are voluntarily dismissed or settled, the court could consider allowing a replacement candidate to be selected by the side that is not responsible for the elimination of the bellwether case from the pool. Where, for example, plaintiffs voluntarily dismiss a case, defendants could be allowed to pick a replacement bellwether candidate. Similarly, while there is arguably less of a justification for corrective measures in the case of settlement, given that both sides must agree to the settlement and thus such cases are not eliminated in a unilateral fashion, commentators have suggested allowing plaintiffs to replace bellwether candidates that are removed from the pool due to settlement.[174] While such a procedure may provide the appearance of symmetry, it may not be fully justified.

In the *Taxotere* MDL, for example, the court issued an order governing selection of bellwethers that contained provisions authorizing substitutions under certain specific circumstances. The order stated that bellwethers could be removed from the trial pool only for "good cause such as health or critical family matters"; if there were no such good cause for removal, removal would only occur if the plaintiff dismissed the claim with prejudice.[175] Where plaintiff counsel removed a potential bellwether from the pool without good cause, the defendants were authorized to pick a substitute plaintiff. In the case of settlement of a trial pool case, the court's order provided that, "the parties shall meet and confer and submit joint or competing proposals to the Court regarding replacement or other relief."[176] Accordingly, the court did not treat settlement of a bellwether case in a parallel or symmetrical fashion, but rather recognized that settlement is really a joint decision on the part of plaintiffs and defendants; thus, any replacement of a bellwether resulting from settlement should be made jointly.

MDL courts have also experimented with combining these selection procedures to come up with hybrid selection processes. For example, MDL courts may select a certain number of cases randomly while allowing the parties to select the remainder of the bellwether picks. The court may employ random selection and then allow the parties to exercise strikes. The court may employ procedures to ensure that cases falling within certain categories are selected, while employing other mechanisms, such as party selection or random selection, to populate these different categories. The court may select certain cases itself and then allow the parties to pick the rest.

In short, there are many possible permutations and combinations that can be employed in implementing the bellwether selection process. However, there is general acknowledgment that the theoretical goal of the process is to obtain a representative sample from the inventory of cases filed in the MDL proceeding. Courts continue to experiment with such procedures in an effort to make the bellwether process as representative as possible. To that end, regardless of the particular selection procedure employed, increasing the amount of information available to the court and the parties regarding the universe of potential claims frequently improves the representativeness of the selections. After all, such knowledge is necessary if one wants to judge the representativeness of the cases that are ultimately picked using the particular selection mechanisms employed in the MDL proceeding.

Location of Bellwether Trials

Another aspect of the bellwether process that receives less attention is the forum in which the cases are tried. One artifact of an MDL proceeding is that the trials typically occur in a single jurisdiction before the same judge. This result may be particularly contrary to what the drafters of the MDL statute contemplated, given that the statute was focused on pre-trial proceedings and not the trial of cases. There is a great diversity in terms of jury pools across this country. A Nashville jury is likely not the same as a San Francisco or Philadelphia jury. Accordingly, holding bellwether trials all in a single jurisdiction is not particularly representative of cases that, in fact, may have been transferred from all over the country. Many of these cases no doubt would have much different outcomes if they were tried in the jurisdiction from which they were transferred, as opposed to the jurisdiction in which the MDL is established.

This aspect of MDL practice therefore leads to results that may not be representative—at least representative of what would happen with the claims if they were litigated individually throughout the country. The general practice in MDL proceedings is to continue to try bellwethers in a single jurisdiction before a single judge. This may be the result of inertia, the fact that trying cases in other locations may be inefficient and more costly, or a desire by the MDL court to maintain control over the litigation.

The MDL court certainly has the authority, however, to have trials held in other jurisdictions. The MDL statute specifically contemplates that cases may be remanded to the transferor jurisdictions for trial. Accordingly, MDL courts could experiment with holding trials in other jurisdictions. This would allow the court and the parties to get some sense of outcomes in other jurisdictions. It would also give the parties an opportunity to see how another judge might view the cases. And, to some extent, it might be an antidote to the defense bar criticism of bellwether trials—that they can be a powerful incentive to settle where the MDL is established in an outlier jurisdiction that may result in more frequent or larger plaintiff verdicts.

Moreover, as noted previously, to the extent the MDL judge wants to continue presiding over the trials, the court may attempt to implement an inter-circuit transfer. This would eliminate the potential benefit of having new judges conduct trials, but to the extent the MDL judge believes there is greater benefit to having the MDL judge continue to preside over bellwether trials, this procedure would allow the judge to do so. The fact that such procedures are not more common, however, demonstrates that there appears to be resistance to innovation in this area.

Coordination Among Plaintiff Counsel

Politics among the law firms representing plaintiffs in an MDL may skew the bellwether process. The lead plaintiff firms the MDL court has appointed to be members of the Plaintiff Executive Committee may exert undue influence over the selection of bellwether cases. Eager to participate in any trials in the MDL proceeding, the committee members may tend to favor their own cases even if they are not the best ones to try or representative of the larger universe of claims.

As Professor Chamblee Burch discusses in her book, such disputes spilled out into the public domain in the *General Motors Ignition Switch* litigation. There, certain executive committee members were criticized strongly for selecting their own cases, even though those cases were weaker ones that some plaintiff counsel believed should not have been tried and which resulted in defense verdicts that hurt all plaintiffs in the litigation. Indeed, one prominent plaintiff lawyer suggested the court should change the membership of the executive committee based on this track record.[177]

This episode only underscores that the selection of bellwether cases may not always be based on representativeness, or even logical considerations. Rather, there may be other factors that can significantly influence which cases end up being tried. In addition to internal politics, selections may be the result of poor or limited research on the pool of cases by one side or the other. Also, one must remember that the selection process is run by human beings who do not always have perfect information. There are many moving parts in any individual case that can be relevant to the strength of the claims. It is difficult to assess such factors in any individual case, much less attempt to assess such factors in thousands of pending cases. Nonetheless, while bellwether selection will never be a perfect process, there are procedures parties have used successfully in prior MDLs to attempt to improve the representativeness of the cases selected for trial.

Multi-Plaintiff Trials

Criticisms of the bellwether process have been especially strong with respect to the few MDLs in which the court has allowed consolidated trials involving multiple plaintiffs. Critics of such trials argue that they provide non-representative results due to juror confusion caused by trying different cases with different facts in a single trial. Consolidation of cases for trial is particularly inappropriate where the cases raise significant issues "in an area of scientific inquiry such as medicine, where . . . scientific and legal controversies are impacted by many individualized circumstances and conditions."[178] This is typical in mass tort cases, where there are usually many significant scientific and medical issues regarding causation, for example.

Such multi-plaintiff trials may also be inappropriate and non-representative because they tend to magnify the appearance of the alleged problem by presenting multiple individuals to the jury who all allege the same or similar injury as a result of defendants' conduct. This is particularly true where claims brought by those who are significantly injured are paired with claims by individuals who have not suffered serious injuries. The presence of the significantly injured plaintiff may elevate the recovery of all of the plaintiffs in a consolidated trial. For these reasons and others, defense groups have argued that, "the use of multi-plaintiff trials as a means of assessing the overall value of a litigation in the MDL context is inherently unreliable and inappropriate."[179]

Indeed, while plaintiffs have requested such consolidations, they are a rarity in modern MDL practice. Most courts recognize that if one party objects to an unusual procedural device, as is the case with defendants in the case of consolidation for trial, pressing forward with such procedures will render the bellwether process less valuable.

The parties will not be satisfied with a process they view as flawed. Nor will they view verdicts reached through such a process as a reliable measure of the value of the asserted claims. Accordingly, just as it does not make sense to select individual cases that are not representative of the general population in an MDL proceeding, it likewise makes little sense to employ procedures, such as trial consolidation, that one side or the other will view as inherently leading to flawed and unreliable results.

Such concerns have led commentators to recommend against consolidated trials in the context of MDL proceedings. Illustrative of this growing consensus are the Duke guidelines, which state: "Cases should generally not be consolidated for trial. At the bellwether stage, the goal should be to achieve valid tests, not to resolve large numbers of claims. Consolidation can tilt the playing field, undermining the goal of producing representative verdicts."[180] Mindful of such recommendations, with few exceptions, the trend is away from such procedural devices.

Utility of the Bellwether Process

In the final analysis, however, one must make an assessment regarding how useful the bellwether process is at all. Arguably, the primary way in which an MDL can contribute to the efficient resolution of litigation is by weeding out the cases that are not valid through pretrial procedures—not conducting sample trials. One-off trials that are frequently not representative of the general population of claims do not provide much basis for progress toward resolution of the litigation. To move toward settlement, it may be necessary to try more cases than the MDL court has tolerance for and in a greater number of jurisdictions than is typical in an MDL proceeding. This is increasingly true as defendants become more skeptical of the bellwether process. Moreover, as defendants frequently note, where settlements do occur after bellwether trials, it is frequently through coercion. The bellwether process can have adverse effects on the litigation by compelling settlement of cases that should not result in settlement or increasing the amount of settlement to levels that are not warranted. Accordingly, the costs of the bellwether process may outweigh any associated benefits.

In the future, courts may increasingly undertake an analysis to determine whether a bellwether process actually would be beneficial for the litigation. Indeed, the Duke guidelines specifically note that such analysis is a best practice in MDL proceedings. There may be cases where, for example, the claims are so individualized that a bellwether process does not provide useful information. Similarly, there may be instances in which one side or the other may believe bellwethers simply will not be representative or useful for encouraging settlement. There also may be instances where the merits are so dubious that it makes sense to resolve pre-trial motions before getting bogged down in work preparing for bellwether trials that may never occur if the claims are all dismissed. In such circumstances, it may make sense to put greater focus on pre-trial motion practice and then remand any remaining cases to the courts from which they were transferred.

Accordingly, it is likely that in the future, increasing scrutiny will be given to the bellwether process in general. Moreover, courts may give additional thought to whether it makes sense to craft the schedule in a way that takes into account the potential that a bellwether process may turn out to be unnecessary or may appear unwarranted depending on other developments in the litigation during the pre-trial phase.

8
Settlement

The accepted wisdom is that a large majority of cases in MDL proceedings are settled, rather than resolved through litigation. Indeed, only a few years ago the Federal Judicial Center noted: "Experience shows that MDL proceedings, like most civil cases, usually do end in settlement. Indeed, an MDL provides an extremely favorable structure for resolution. Where settlements are reasonable and just, they stand as a testament to the effectiveness of the MDL process."[181] While some view settlement as an indication of the success of MDL proceedings, as noted in prior chapters, others are highly critical of this orientation of some MDL courts. Despite these differences, both critics and supporters appear to agree that a number of MDL courts in fact view their role as facilitating global settlement: "[T]he 'settlement culture' for which the federal courts are so frequently criticized is nowhere more prevalent than in MDL practice."[182]

The fact of centralization in MDL proceedings alone encourages settlement. An MDL brings the parties together in a common forum in which the court can provide a larger degree of certainty regarding how the litigation will proceed and provides opportunities for communication and coordination among the parties. Indeed, as a standard practice in MDL proceedings, MDL courts generally develop a structure for coordination among the plaintiffs' lawyers involved in the case, which may facilitate settlement negotiations. As the Federal Judicial Center has noted, "[o]ne of the values of MDL proceedings is that they bring before a single judge all of the federal cases, parties, and counsel making up the litigation. They therefore afford a unique opportunity for the negotiation of a global settlement."[183]

Nonetheless, as demonstrated in prior chapters, many MDL proceedings have been effectively resolved through judicial rulings on dispositive motions or other mechanisms for addressing the merits of the claims. Settlement plays no role, or a less significant role, in such MDL proceedings. Moreover, such approaches appear to be increasingly common, as courts recognize the need to resolve the key issues in the MDL and address claims that lack merit before any negotiated resolution can be achieved.

Indeed, even where motion practice or other litigation procedures do not completely resolve the litigation, they can have a profound effect on any subsequent settlement. Rulings by the MDL court may dramatically change settlement values even where the court does not eliminate all or a significant portion of the claims through dispositive rulings. In fact, in many cases, before settlement is feasible it is necessary for the MDL court to provide guidance regarding the scope of potential liability by ruling on dispositive motions.

Despite the recent successes of courts that have used this traditional model of adjudication to resolve large MDL proceedings, there are MDLs in which courts are focused almost exclusively on settlement. One widely cited example is the massive MDL addressing claims against the manufacturers of prescription opioids. Academic commentators frequently note that, from the very beginning of the proceedings, the federal judge presiding over the MDL encouraged the parties to develop a settlement that would abate the opioid crisis.[184] Commentators have cited such examples in arguing that some MDL proceedings are really more akin to administrative or regulatory proceedings, rather than traditional adversarial litigation.[185] Under this conception of the MDL process, judges are viewed as problem-solvers, rather than neutral arbiters, who employ flexible procedures to address the unique facts and circumstances of pressing societal problems. However, this model is certainly not consistent with traditional forms of litigation in our adversarial system, much less the statutory and rule-based framework governing MDL proceedings.

More generally, there are examples of MDL proceedings in which settlements occurred before the MDL court had done anything to assess the merits of the underlying claims in any meaningful way. Professor Elizabeth Chamblee Burch reports that in the MDL proceedings she reviewed, "38% of transferee judges had not ruled on summary judgment motions, 32% had not decided *Daubert* motions, and 55.8% had not presided over bellwether trials."[186] In her view, this is a particularly troublesome phenomenon given that, "[w]hen judges don't engage with the merits through pretrial motions and trials, the relative strength of plaintiffs' cases may matter little in settlement negotiations."[187] Such outcomes may not only disadvantage plaintiffs whose claims are more meritorious than those of the average plaintiff in the claimant population, but they also support the contentions of defendants who maintain that some MDLs have devolved into a mechanism for coercing settlements, regardless of the merits of the underlying claims.

Professor Burch cites the *Pradaxa* MDL as an example of this sort of pattern in which MDL courts have taken an aggressive approach to encouraging settlement. In *Pradaxa*, plaintiffs alleged that a blood thinner used to treat patients with atrial fibrillation could cause bleeding events and that there was no adequate treatment to stop the bleeding when it occurred. The MDL court issued a series of discovery rulings sanctioning the manufacturer; however, it did not hold any bellwether trials or otherwise address the merits. Rather, it took a series of steps to attempt to induce the parties to settle, culminating in the court calling the parties before it to ask them "why the proceeding hadn't yet settled," ordering lawyers with settlement authority to appear before the court, and presiding over a mediation process that resulted in a $650 million settlement.[188] This all occurred in a case where the complication at issue was a known side effect of the drug and the scientific and medical communities had concluded that the significant benefits of this class of medication outweighed the known risk of bleeding events.

While such examples may be outliers, they do show that some MDL courts apparently take a different approach when presiding over multidistrict litigation as compared with individual civil lawsuits: "Most judges concede that they would never use the same tactics in a typical civil suit."[189] This is certainly a potential red flag for parties involved in multidistrict litigation. The approach to multidistrict litigation arguably should be no different than that in individual cases, given that the same rules of procedure apply equally to both proceedings. However, some courts apparently are of the view that something more is needed to resolve large MDL cases involving multiple lawyers and multiple claims. The question arises whether such measures are, in fact, warranted and whether they exceed the bounds of the proper role of courts in the federal system.

As illustrated in the examples found in prior chapters, many MDL courts have taken the opposite approach, successfully adopting a traditional adversarial model to resolve large-scale multidistrict litigation that is not focused solely on achieving a global settlement. Indeed, the traditional adversarial approach in which claims are litigated under the normal rules of civil procedure is arguably the most successful model courts have followed in MDL proceedings.

However, even where courts follow the traditional model, to a greater or lesser degree, settlement is a potential outcome in each MDL and, as we will see, there are many different approaches to settlement in such proceedings. There is obviously a range in how comprehensive any settlement in an MDL will be given that such proceedings may involve hundreds or thousands of individual claims brought by many different lawyers. Settlements may range from a settlement in an individual case that has been consolidated in the MDL proceeding, to global settlements that encompass all of the individual cases that are consolidated in the proceeding, or something in between. Likewise, there are different degrees to which the court or third parties may be involved in the settlement process. Depending on the unique circumstances of each MDL, different models of settlement may be more appropriate in different proceedings.

The Role of the MDL Court

As noted in prior chapters, defendants have observed that aggregation of claims in an MDL proceeding can produce enormous pressure to settle the litigation. The risk of litigating such a large number of claims can be significant. This is even more true where the MDL court fails to take an active role in eliminating claims that should not have been filed. A defendant may go through an MDL process with little or nothing to show for it except for mounting litigation costs. Accordingly, from the defendants' perspective, there are inherent pressures in an MDL setting that may result in settlements that are not just or equitable.

However, these are not the only criticisms that have been leveled at the settlement process in the context of MDL proceedings. Advocates for plaintiffs have suggested that there is a potential for what amounts to collusion between the lead plaintiff counsel in charge of the litigation and defendants, whereby lead counsel may negotiate increased fees for themselves at the expense of non-lead counsel or even plaintiffs themselves: "For example, in *Guidant, Vioxx*, and the *Genetically Modified Rice Litigation*, lead lawyers inserted terms into global settlements that increased their fees and required settling plaintiffs to waive their fee objections if they wanted to enroll in the settlement."[190]

Moreover, critics sometimes note the lack of procedural guarantees that ensure the fairness of settlements in MDL proceedings, particularly when compared with class action settlements under Rule 23 of the Federal Rules of Civil Procedure. Under Rule 23, courts approve a class settlement "after a hearing and only on finding that it is fair, reasonable, and adequate."[191] While there is a range in terms of the extensiveness of the inquiry, in the context of Rule 23 there is at least a formal, rule-based structure for review of the fairness of a proposed settlement. Some critics of MDL settlement lament the lack of formalized procedures applicable to such settlements akin to those that apply to class action settlements under Rule 23.

Other critics offer a somewhat opposite critique. Consistent with the view that defendants are under undue pressure to settle MDL proceedings, some have expressed concern that judges in MDL proceedings may become too involved with settlement discussions and may add to the pressure on defendants to settle. They point to examples such as the *Pradaxa* MDL and others where courts have adopted the more active model of judicial involvement in settlement negotiations.[192]

In an extreme situation, an overly active role by the judge in settlement discussions may result in requests for recusal in the event that settlement talks fail. This problem can arise where the judge learns confidential information during the course of the settlement negotiations. Even where no party seeks recusal, "[j]udges who have been involved in unsuccessful settlement negotiations sometimes turn over to another judge the responsibility for trying the case because they have been privy to information on the merits of the case or on issues that would otherwise not have been revealed."[193] The result of recusal in an MDL could be significant given the extensive involvement of the judge in such all-consuming litigation. If the judge were forced to recuse, all of that experience would be lost. Accordingly, "[i]n mass torts, as in other types of complex litigation, questions regarding the appropriate extent of judicial involvement in settlement negotiations are important because the costs associated with recusal of a judge familiar with the litigation are high."[194]

MDL judges thus walk something of a tightrope with a lack of clear principles or rules guiding their actions and with critics on both sides suggesting somewhat inconsistent approaches. The Duke guidelines illustrate this divide, suggesting that, "[i]f the parties indicate a willingness to negotiate settlement, the MDL judge should facilitate negotiations, but judges should not impose settlement negotiations on unwilling parties."[195] However, the guidelines further recognize the need for some oversight role for the court in ensuring the fairness and transparency of global settlements, noting that, "[f]or global settlements, which will resolve an entire MDL, the court should ensure the integrity and transparency of the process that led to the settlement agreement, including the claims process."[196]

Such concerns, along with the natural proclivities of the judge, lead to a fairly wide range in terms of the degree of participation of the judge in settlement negotiations: "Although some judges participate actively in settlement negotiations, others insulate themselves from the negotiations, leaving this activity to a magistrate judge, a special master, or a settlement judge."[197] Accordingly, third parties may engage in settlement activities in parallel with the litigation proceedings.

This approach reduces some of the concerns associated with a more active judicial role in settlement proceedings. Relying on a third party removes the MDL judge from the negotiations. It also addresses to some extent concerns that the involvement of the judge may put pressure on the parties to settle. However, it does not necessarily provide plaintiffs with any greater protections. The fact of the matter is that, where the parties voluntarily agree to settlement terms and there is no formal mechanism for court involvement, it is difficult to implement such protections in the settlement process. Nonetheless, a greater degree of transparency in how cases are settled in MDL proceedings might improve the process.

Others have suggested that the court consider becoming involved in administering the settlement after the parties have concluded their negotiations. Even if the court plays a limited, or no, role in the negotiation of the settlement agreement, it may play an important role after agreement is reached. For example, the Duke guidelines state: "If the parties reach an agreement to resolve all or a substantial portion of the cases, and the parties so request, the court should be prepared to take an ongoing role in implementing and enforcing the settlement agreement."[198]

However, MDL courts do not always take such an active role. They do not typically involve themselves extensively in the distribution of settlement funds among the plaintiffs. Nor do they assess the fairness of settlement, unless the MDL contains class actions that require an analysis under Rule 23. Accordingly, the role of the judge with respect to settlement remains relatively traditional in this regard.

Nor is there much in the way of transparency in MDL proceedings. As noted, much of the information regarding the distribution of settlement proceeds never sees the light of day. While anecdotal reports indicate that many plaintiffs are simply unable to meet the criteria necessary to receive settlement compensation, data regarding distribution are generally not public. A greater degree of transparency regarding the settlement process might protect plaintiffs while providing valuable information regarding the degree to which plaintiff counsel are submitting claims that lack support in MDL proceedings.

Types of Settlement

There are many different forms in which settlement may occur in an MDL proceeding. In addition to settlement of individual cases that are part of an MDL proceeding, there may also be different types of group settlements that resolve all or some subset of the cases filed in an MDL proceeding. For example, defendants may engage in an inventory settlement that resolves all of the cases brought by a particular law firm. Likewise, there may be settlements that address particular categories of claims, such as those involving a particular injury that is distinct from other alleged injuries at issue in the litigation. Finally, there may be a global settlement in which all plaintiffs may participate, no matter which law firm represents them, which would result in the resolution of the entire MDL proceeding.

However, one commonality in all of these different types of settlements is that defendants face an uncertainty regarding whether settlement really buys them peace. Unlike a class action where all members of the class are bound by a settlement, in an MDL setting the defendants will only be settling the claims of plaintiffs who agree to join the settlement. Defendants may face an ongoing stream of lawsuits even after they settle all of the claims of the plaintiffs before them. All they can do is hope the law firms with which they settle will not turn around and file additional claims against them. Moreover, even if defendants believe these law firms will not recruit new clients to file claims against them, there may be other law firms that have not settled that may see an opening to file new claims. Accordingly, it is difficult in the context of an MDL proceeding to ensure that the litigation will be terminated completely through settlement.

In addition, as noted, in an aggregated proceeding such as an MDL, there is always a concern that defendants may be providing compensation for claims that lack merit at the expense of more meritorious claims. In the context of a class action settlement, the court is required to inquire into the fairness of the settlement to protect the rights of absent class members. In an MDL proceeding, no such requirement exists, and some critics of the MDL process believe that plaintiffs themselves have suffered as a result.

The parties in MDL proceedings have developed mechanisms to try to address these problems. For example, in large global settlements the parties typically implement a grid arrangement that seeks to compensate claimants who have more significant injuries at greater rates than those who do not. Similarly, as noted, global settlements typically build in criteria that must be met to receive compensation to attempt to address the problem of invalid claims. However, these are imprecise measures that do not necessarily ensure that plaintiffs with more significant claims receive substantially greater compensation. Rather, to some extent, they balance ease of administration with accurate valuation of claims. In addition, as we have seen, they may lead to windfall recoveries on behalf of plaintiff counsel who on paper may represent many more claimants than those who actually would receive compensation under the criteria of the global settlement.[199]

In addition, such global settlements typically contain provisions designed to maximize participation in the settlement to at least provide some measure of assurance for defendants that they will buy peace with respect to existing claims.[200] Such settlements generally require that a certain percentage of the plaintiff population accept the settlement before it goes into effect. In addition, the settlements may contain provisions that require lawyers to recommend to their clients that they accept the settlement terms. As commentators have observed, such provisions have been incorporated into a number of large pharmaceutical MDL settlements: "After first being used in the *Propulsid* MDL, [such provisions] reappeared in the *Vioxx*, *Fosamax*, and *Yasmin/Yaz* MDLs."[201]

Plaintiff advocates have also observed that the court may play a significant role in attempting to ensure that a global settlement is truly global. According to some commentators, the premium MDL judges place on settlement may lead them to suggest to plaintiffs considering whether to join in the global settlement that, if they do not accept the settlement, the judge will dismiss their cases: "[O]nce a judge decides a deal is fair, her subsequent orders can send a firm message: settle or I'll dismiss your case."[202]

While they may facilitate settlement, commentators have expressed concern with such tactics: "When judges use their power to approve, enforce, and push plaintiffs into private settlements . . . they not only appear to exceed the authority that rightly belongs to them, they may impinge on plaintiffs' free will to consent."[203] Moreover, commentators have observed that such tactics may be more likely in circumstances where the court lacks full information regarding the claims and may be subject to a form of capture by the plaintiff lawyers on the leadership committee who are promoting the settlement. According to these commentators, depending on the court's level of involvement and engagement in the litigation prior to the settlement, the court may be subject to a greater or lesser degree of influence by the lawyers promoting the settlement. As a result, plaintiff lawyers who are not on the executive committee, and therefore do not have as great a level of access to the MDL court, may find it difficult to resist settlement of their clients' claims.[204]

One potential counter-argument to such concerns, however, is that the plaintiffs who seek to avoid settlement may simply be hold-outs who are seeking to extract more compensation than is warranted for their claims. Indeed, many of these cases may, in fact, lack any merit at all. The data discussed in prior chapters illustrate that many of the claims in an MDL are flawed in one way or the other and that, even under the relatively non-rigorous criteria imposed by most settlements, they may not be eligible for settlement payments. There are benefits to global settlement for all plaintiffs who will receive compensation, and these hold-out plaintiffs may be acting in ways that, on average, are to the general detriment of plaintiffs who have filed claims in the litigation.

Ironically, courts seeking to impose a global settlement may begin to suggest that they will apply procedures to assess the merits of the claims to the stragglers that they did not apply before a global settlement was reached. Thus, for example, in addition to suggesting that opt-out cases may not survive motions to dismiss, courts may also adopt procedures such as *Lone Pine* orders to require plaintiffs to submit independent expert opinions that support their claims. Such tactics only reinforce that such procedures could have been employed at the outset of the litigation to address the merits *before* settlement. Nonetheless, such procedures represent one more tool in the toolbox for settlement-oriented judges who wish to enforce a global settlement that concludes the litigation in its entirety.

Class Settlement

In some cases, the dynamics of class settlement may overlap with MDL settlement. Some MDL proceedings may contain cases that are purported class actions or, indeed, may be comprised entirely of class action cases. In such circumstances, where there is a class-wide settlement, the court must adhere to the requirements of Rule 23: "In a settlement context, the proposed class must meet Rule 23 requirements, with the exception of trial manageability, and the court must carefully review the proposed settlement terms to ensure that they are fair, reasonable, and adequate."[205]

The procedural requirements for class certification are well-defined and specified by rule. The court must inquire into the fairness of the settlement to ensure that the due process rights of absent class members are protected. This generally entails fairly extensive hearings. Potential objectors may oppose the settlement on various grounds, and the court will then have to resolve the objections. Indeed, there are professional objectors who may challenge the fairness of proposed class action settlements and, in some cases, such objections may be less than meritorious. In sum, a class settlement generally entails a greater amount of work for the court and the parties to ensure that the requirements of Rule 23 are met and to address any potential objections to settlement.

Moreover, in a pair of decisions, *Amchem Products, Inc. v. Windsor*[206] and *Ortiz v. Fibreboard Corp.*,[207] the Supreme Court limited the availability of the class action device to resolve the sort of large mass tort litigation that is frequently the subject of MDL proceedings today. In those decisions, the Court noted that the individual differences and conflicts among members of the class made the class action device inappropriate in the context of mass tort claims. In *Amchem*, for example, the Court held that certification of a class asserting asbestos personal injury claims was inappropriate because, among other things, the class members were exposed to different asbestos-containing products, in different ways, over different periods, and for different amounts of time, resulting in disabling disease for some plaintiffs and no physical injury for others.[208] Moreover, the Court concluded that the "the interests of those within the . . . class are not aligned," given that "currently injured" plaintiffs sought "generous immediate payments" whereas "exposure-only" plaintiffs sought "an ample, inflation-protected fund for the future."[209] The Court in *Ortiz* rejected a settlement class comprised of asbestos personal injury claimants for similar reasons, noting the "divergent interests of the presently injured and future claimants" created conflicts that made class certification inappropriate.[210]

Despite this precedent, as commentators have noted, there have been recent efforts to use the class action device in novel ways to achieve global settlements in MDLs that completely resolve the litigation: "MDL catalyzed the reemergence of settlement class actions that [the Supreme Court's decisions in] *Amchem* and *Ortiz* appeared to bar. Reasoning that mega-MDLs provide structural guarantees of fairness missing in *Amchem* and *Ortiz*, courts approved class settlement notwithstanding conflicts of interests that those cases suggested could only be addressed through subclassing."[211]

One of the more unusual attempts at utilizing the class action device in the context of multidistrict litigation occurred in the *National Prescription Opiate* litigation. There, the judge certified a negotiation class of local government entities suing the manufacturers of opioids in a massive MDL proceeding. While critics of the procedure questioned what precisely such a class would accomplish, it appears the intent of the class was to authorize certain lawyers to negotiate on behalf of all plaintiffs with the manufacturer defendants. However, in the event a settlement were reached, the members of the class would have to agree to the settlement. Accordingly, as a practical matter, it is unclear that certifying a negotiation class will lead to meaningful progress toward resolution of cases in an MDL. Indeed, most of the state attorneys general involved in the opioid litigation opposed the concept. They objected to any attempt by counties or cities that filed claims in the litigation to participate in the proposed negotiation class and ultimately an appellate court decertified the class.[212]

While many object to the use of the class action procedure in this fashion, some have observed that class action practice may at least provide some guidance to improve the fairness of MDL settlements. They argue that there is the potential the class action or other similar procedural devices might provide "a vehicle for judicial involvement in settlement of an MDL proceeding" without formal amendment of the rules of civil procedure.[213] At a minimum, such procedural moves are a recognition that something is lacking in terms of the procedures for settlement in MDL proceedings. This is an area that may receive increasing attention in the coming years.

Parallel Proceedings

There are a variety of factors that can make settlement of an MDL proceeding more difficult. One of these is the presence of significant state court proceedings running in parallel with the federal MDL. To the extent litigation is dispersed with different groups of plaintiff counsel running the various clusters of cases, it becomes more difficult to reach a global resolution of the litigation. Indeed, in many instances the presence of significant state court proceedings is the result of a conscious decision by the lawyers involved. They file in state court precisely because they want to remain in state court and pursue litigation in that forum independently of any MDL proceeding. These lawyers may have a very different agenda and very different views than lawyers who actively seek to participate in MDL proceedings, which are notoriously oriented toward achieving a global settlement of all claims.

The Federal Judicial Center has recognized the difficulties that parallel state court litigation can present. It has expressed the view that "[c]oordination of mediation or settlement efforts is particularly important when there are pending state court cases related to the MDL cases. State and federal judges should encourage joint comprehensive settlement negotiations and alternative dispute resolution procedures."[214] As with litigating state claims in parallel, in attempting to settle state litigation in parallel, coordination is important.

However, it may not be possible to achieve one global settlement that resolves both MDL and state court litigation. It may be necessary to attempt piecemeal settlements. Just as sometimes it is necessary (or desirable) to attempt to achieve inventory settlements with certain law firms instead of one overarching global settlement, so, too, it is sometimes necessary to pursue piecemeal settlement with firms in the MDL and in the parallel state court proceedings.

To some extent this occurred in the *Heparin* litigation, for example.[215] There, the parties reached a settlement in the federal litigation shortly after most of the claims were eliminated through summary judgment proceedings on common issues. No bellwether trials occurred in the federal MDL proceedings, as certain bellwethers were eliminated based on flaws in the plaintiffs' claims in those cases. However, plaintiffs continued to litigate claims in a consolidated Illinois state court proceeding. There, plaintiffs did attempt to try bellwethers in a state court venue before a state court jury in Chicago. However, after the plaintiffs ended up receiving much less than they anticipated in the one test case that went to trial, a settlement of that litigation soon followed.

To the extent the discipline of MDL proceedings continues to erode and there is a proliferation of parallel state court proceedings, it may be increasingly difficult to achieve global settlements. The recent disputes involving the weed killer Roundup, opioids, and talc provide examples illustrating the difficulty of achieving a global resolution of litigation where there is significant and dispersed state court litigation. While a global resolution ultimately may be achieved, in the meantime the litigation is protracted with cases tried in both state and federal courts without a negotiated settlement that resolves the litigation in its entirety. Rather, settlement is constrained to individual cases, and a variety of factors continue to frustrate settlement on a more global basis.

Potential Conflicts Among Plaintiff Counsel

More generally, settlement can raise the issue of potential conflicts within the plaintiff's bar, including among plaintiff firms that are all pursuing their claims in the MDL. Indeed, in MDL proceedings, "questions are frequently raised with respect to Lead Counsel's role in negotiating both inventory settlements on behalf of their own clients that may disfavor other plaintiffs and global settlements that disfavor their own clients."[216]

For example, concerns may be raised where one of the plaintiff firms serving on a leadership committee enters into negotiations with defendants to execute an inventory settlement that would settle that firm's cases. The firms that serve on the leadership committee have agreed to undertake work on behalf of all plaintiffs in the litigation. By virtue of their position, theoretically, they may be able to extract a premium for their cases in unilateral settlement discussions to the extent defendants believe there is some value to be gained from removing one of these firms from the litigation. This possibility may be more theoretical than real, given that there are other firms on these committees and more lawyers in the wings ready to step in. Nonetheless, there have been debates regarding the ethics of such settlement negotiations, with some arguing that, "before engaging in 'inventory' settlement negotiations, Lead Counsel should resign."[217]

Similarly, as highlighted previously, the lawyers serving on the leadership committees and those who are not may have different interests when it comes to negotiating a global settlement. The lawyers on the leadership committees have a significant interest in global settlement, given that they will extract a percentage of the settlement value from *all* the cases in the MDL proceeding in the form of common benefit fees. In contrast, there may be some plaintiff counsel who believe the compensation their clients will receive in a global settlement is too low and they could do better for themselves and their clients if cases were remanded to the transferor courts and were individually litigated. Indeed, in some cases these lawyers may not be in federal court on a voluntary basis. Rather, they may have filed their cases in state court and had them removed to federal court by the defendants.

Accordingly, there are a number of potential practical and ethical considerations that must be taken into account with respect to settlement in the context of an MDL proceeding. The potential conflicts that exist within the plaintiff bar can result in significant disruption in the proceedings, frustrating settlement or leading to other adverse consequences. In the *General Motors Ignition Switch* litigation, for example, when plaintiff counsel sought the removal of one of the leadership members, they cited not only his conduct with respect to bellwether selection, but also his negotiation of a separate inventory settlement with General Motors that the lawyers maintained was at odds with the interests of the other plaintiffs in the litigation.[218] The relationship between the leadership and the rest of the lawyers pursuing claims in an MDL can pose significant problems for the efficient administration of an MDL proceeding.

Attorneys' Fees

Finally, where the parties have reached a settlement, the court must determine whether and to what extent to scrutinize the fees received by the attorneys representing the plaintiffs in the proceeding. As one judge who has presided over multiple MDL proceedings has written, "it is important to recognize that judicial review of the fee arrangements of the attorneys appearing before the court is not only controversial but unpleasant. Some courts have concluded that this comes with the territory and have occasionally found it necessary to wade into this Serbonian Bog."[219]

In reviewing attorney fees, the court may invoke its general authority to oversee the administration of a settlement or the conduct of the lawyers before the court. The court may apply multiple measures to determine whether the fees are reasonable. This can include examining the percentage recovery under the contingent fee relationship, a lodestar method that calculates the reasonable value of the number of hours the lawyers spent pursuing the litigation, or a blended method that compares the two calculations.

Not surprisingly, attorneys in MDL litigation generally are not thrilled with the prospect of the court reviewing their fee arrangements for reasonableness. As we have seen, there are circumstances where the lawyers may receive a windfall under the settlement agreement. Having presided over the MDL case, the judge is in a good position to assess whether the fees received by the lawyers are somehow inequitable or unreasonable under the circumstances. Given the debate regarding the compensation of attorneys, and in particular those in leadership in large MDL proceedings, we may see increasing scrutiny of the fee arrangements of the attorneys participating in such litigation.

9
What Can Go Wrong

As the criticisms of the MDL process discussed in prior chapters suggest, there are a number of things that can go wrong, and have gone wrong, in MDL proceedings. As a result, there have been a number of proposed reforms to the rules and statutes that govern MDL practice. Nonetheless, a survey of MDL proceedings demonstrates that the problems that have arisen cannot always be addressed by rule or statute. It further demonstrates that, in many instances, MDL courts have used the existing rules effectively to resolve large-scale MDL proceedings. Either through motion practice or administrative order, diligent application of the normal rules governing litigation in the federal courts can go a long way to effectively resolving even the most complicated MDL proceedings. Nonetheless, given the problems that have occurred, there is likely to be ongoing discussion regarding proposals for reform.

Dissatisfaction with the Process for Selecting the MDL Judge

One of the recurring criticisms of MDL procedure is that it vests a significant amount of power in the judge presiding over the litigation. This is unavoidable in the context of an MDL proceeding. The efficiency of an MDL proceeding is largely due to the fact that it is run by a single decision maker. However, as with any set of procedures, there are costs associated with this type of system. One of those costs is the potential risk associated with a single decision maker making key decisions that will potentially govern thousands of cases.

In an MDL proceeding, a single judge issues rulings that may be applicable to all cases, supplanting the normal process where judges around the country decide the same or similar issues, providing differing perspectives on the central aspects of the case. Diversity in perspective and potentially outcome are replaced by uniformity. The single forum can also have a significant impact in terms of the jury pool. As noted previously, to the extent there are bellwether trials, there can be a significant bias due to the transfer of all cases to a single forum with a single jury pool.

The dissatisfaction with the model of a single decision maker becomes even greater where the parties are dissatisfied with the process of selection of the MDL judge. As noted in prior chapters, the selection process is governed by a Panel of Article III judges who are charged with deciding which judicial district should receive a new MDL, but who, in practice, actually select the judge who will receive the litigation. While the Panel has articulated a variety of factors that guide its decision making in this regard, and the parties have input into the process, frequently the decision making regarding choice of forum for the MDL is shrouded in mystery.

Moreover, this process is potentially subject to gamesmanship. Plaintiffs may seek to direct an MDL proceeding to a certain district by filing a group of cases in that district while waiting to file elsewhere, leading the Panel to send the litigation to a district where there is already a critical mass of cases.[220] To the extent the system allows one side to unilaterally influence the selection of the MDL judge, confidence in the impartiality of the selection procedure may be eroded. More generally, to the extent there is a lack of transparency in the selection process, it may undermine confidence in an MDL proceeding.

Where the parties lack confidence in the procedures utilized for selection of the decision maker, for whatever reasons, the process can be undermined. Dissatisfaction may extend to the court's rulings, and the parties may be reluctant to raise certain issues with the court. They also may resist trials before the MDL court and may not execute *Lexecon* waivers at the outset of the proceedings. They may be reluctant to allow the MDL to serve as a platform for settlement and may decide that it is preferable to wait for remand of the litigation to the transferor courts, rather than seeking to resolve the litigation in the context of the MDL proceeding.

The responsibility for ensuring that there is a process for selection of the MDL judge rests largely with the Judicial Panel on Multidistrict Litigation, which makes this decision. Generally, the JPML receives competing recommendations from the parties regarding the judges they would like to see presiding over the MDL. However, even though there may be a good basis for selecting the parties' recommended judges based on the factors the Panel considers, the JPML does not always select a judge the parties have proposed. Moreover, the selection process frequently is characterized by a lack of transparency that may lead to dissatisfaction with the selection.

The Panel can avoid this problem with the MDL process by making selections that will be acceptable to the parties that will participate in the MDL. The Panel can endeavor to avoid selecting judges who are unacceptable to one side or the other. The Panel can also endeavor to select judges who have presided over prior MDLs in which the parties were satisfied with the outcome or can reach out to expand the participation of judges to new judges who have reputations of being competent and not biased toward one side or the other in the types of cases that will be centralized in the MDL. In sum, many of the problems associated with selection of the MDL judge can be avoided by thoughtful research undertaken by the Panel when establishing the MDL.

However, there may be room for reform in this area that might mitigate the problem even further. One potential reform would be to afford the parties a certain number of strikes to eliminate potential judicial selections that are under consideration by the Panel. This procedure would function much like the strikes parties employ in eliminating bellwether cases that the other side picks in many MDLs. Moreover, similar procedures are employed in certain state court systems, where the parties are afforded strikes they may exercise to avoid judges who are assigned to their cases. This sort of procedure helps to eliminate the selection of outlier judges who are unacceptable to one side or the other and might increase general satisfaction with the selection process. In any event, given the importance of the selection of the judge who will preside over the MDL, proposals for reform in this area would be welcome.

Lack of Judicial Engagement

Once the MDL proceeding is convened, a critical determinant of the efficiency and effectiveness of the MDL is the willingness of the judge to undertake the hard work necessary to make the proceeding a success. As the Federal Judicial Center has recognized, "[t]he most serious complaint that we ever hear [about MDL proceedings]—though infrequently—is that the judges may not take their MDL responsibilities seriously."[221]

There may be many reasons for such inactivity. For one, confronting thousands of claims that are in many cases somewhat individualized is a daunting task for any judge. While there are many resources to educate judges regarding MDL practices, the challenge is even more significant when the judge is new to the process and has not presided over an MDL proceeding before.

Similarly, in recent years the pressures to achieve a global settlement of large MDL proceedings have become even greater, with an emphasis on attempting to move the MDL quickly.[222] According to some observers, "[t]he Panel views quickly settling a complex case as a hallmark of success that disposes it to reward that judge with new litigation."[223] While moving promptly can have many beneficial effects, the downside occurs where speed comes at the expense of doing the work necessary to ensure that claims are properly evaluated in the MDL proceeding. Moreover, while some judges may be hopeful the parties will settle, settlement may never come. Indeed, the failure of the MDL judge to engage can actually impede settlement. Without judicial rulings on key issues, for example, the parties may not have information necessary to engage in successful settlement negotiations.

Where the judge fails to engage sufficiently with an MDL proceeding, the results can be stagnation and even worse. With respect to generic issues, a failure to engage may lead to allowing litigation to move forward that should not. From the plaintiffs' perspective, however, it is possible that it can also result in broad-brush rulings that may sweep in claims that plaintiffs believe have merit. One way to resolve an MDL proceeding is to grant generic motions, and if one looks at recent MDL proceedings, there seems to be a trend in this direction.

The most frequent result of a lack of engagement is that the individual, case-specific track is neglected. This may be due to a perception that addressing case-specific issues is one of the most time-consuming aspects of multidistrict litigation. Courts that are under significant work and time constraints may hesitate to dive in and begin resolving potentially hundreds or thousands of individual motions. Nonetheless, as noted in prior chapters, the reality is that a little judicial engagement goes a long way, and courts that do engage frequently find that they do not actually need to resolve individual motions in all cases. This is because, once the court begins to rule, it provides guidance to the parties that they can utilize to attempt to resolve issues in other cases off-line without involving the court. Moreover, as noted, case-management procedures can be used to encourage plaintiffs to voluntarily dismiss cases that lack merit without the expenditure of significant judicial resources.

One other potential effect of a lack of judicial engagement is that it may increase settlement pressure even further. Settlement is frequently a costless development for MDL courts. Unlike in a class action setting, courts in MDL proceedings frequently do not engage in significant oversight of resulting settlements. Moreover, a settlement by definition terminates the work the MDL court might otherwise have to perform and saves the MDL court from having to remand large numbers of cases to the court's judicial colleagues in other districts around the country, which is often viewed as a failure.[224] As participants in the MDL process have observed, historically there has been a "sense that an MDL judge has 'failed' if he or she does not broker a litigation-wide settlement because the alternative is to flood federal courts around the country with hundreds or thousands of remanded cases."[225] Accordingly, if the court fails to engage and address the merits of the asserted claims in an MDL proceeding, the only viable option may be to encourage the parties to settle the claims.

Somewhat perversely, however, a lack of judicial engagement motivated by a desire to encourage settlement can actually have the opposite effect. If the court does not undertake the work necessary to adjudicate claims that have been filed in an MDL proceeding, it can actually harm the chances of reaching a negotiated settlement. Defendants are well aware that there is a significant likelihood that many claims filed in an MDL proceeding have received little scrutiny by the lawyers who filed them and may well lack merit. They are aware that many of these claims are generated by lawyer advertising and are encouraged through the use of litigation financing. To the extent the defendants are repeat players, like the pharmaceutical and medical device companies, they are also quite aware that many of the claims that are settled do not even satisfy minimal criteria necessary to qualify for settlement payments. Accordingly, defendants may be unwilling to settle the universe of claims in an MDL proceeding unless there is some scrutiny applied to those claims and there is a better understanding of their validity. A failure to engage in this process in the hope that the parties will settle the case can therefore be counterproductive.

A clear vision of the MDL process at the outset of the proceeding can often help make an MDL run more smoothly and overcome some of these challenges. In this regard, setting a schedule that provides for the efficient resolution of the litigation is critical. A court presiding over an MDL proceeding certainly has a large body of precedent to choose from in crafting the scheduling order. However, as noted in prior chapters, the unique facts and circumstances of each case may influence the provisions in the schedule so the court can address the most critical issues early in the proceeding or emphasize certain aspects of the proceeding over others. In some proceedings, for example, there may be a high likelihood that generic motion practice will be successful, and it may be important to front-load such proceedings. In other proceedings, like the asbestos MDL, it may be that the case-specific issues will dominate. In addition, as discussed previously, in some MDL proceedings bellwether trials may take on great significance, whereas in others a bellwether process may not make much sense.

Accordingly, from the beginning of the MDL proceeding, it is frequently important for the court to have at least some rudimentary understanding of the claims and the nature of the litigation. While schedules can always be modified as circumstances change, preparing a scheduling order is frequently one of the first tasks in an MDL proceeding. In many cases, the court of necessity will have to rely on the parties for an understanding of the claims. At the beginning of the litigation, the parties have superior information regarding the nature of the claims, and the court may rely on them to communicate that information to it. Accordingly, from a practice perspective, it is important for the parties to lay out their view of the merits of the case and the significant issues. Even issues that may seem mundane, such as scheduling, take on added significance in an MDL proceeding and should be viewed as a vehicle for communicating with the court regarding the merits of the claims.

To be in a position to address these issues, it is therefore important for counsel to develop the legal and factual themes they intend to pursue early in the proceeding. Parties in an MDL proceeding likely will be in front of the judge on a regular basis and will be required to begin to articulate the themes they wish to pursue early in the proceedings. To be in a position to articulate these themes, it is necessary to begin a thorough investigation of the facts as early as possible. It is also important in cases involving complicated scientific issues, such as pharmaceutical or product liability cases, to begin researching and understanding the science as early as possible.

Once the parties develop their key themes, they can then communicate them to the judge early in the proceeding. Most MDL judges will likely be eager to learn about the case, and regular status conferences provide an opportunity to educate the judge. The judge may also want to have what have been characterized as "science days" to give the parties an opportunity to present a neutral overview of the scientific issues in the case.[226] While these science days often degenerate into unproductive advocacy, the fact is that lawyers in an MDL proceeding may find themselves having to understand and articulate the key scientific issues early in the proceeding. Such judicial education can help overcome potential problems by showing the judge the path forward with respect to how progress can be made in the MDL.

There may be many other opportunities to educate the judge throughout the MDL proceedings. As we have seen in prior chapters, the MDL process may be viewed as being divided into separate tracks addressing case-specific issues, generic issues, the bellwether process, or other matters. Lessons learned in addressing issues in one of these tracks may influence the court's approach to other tracks.

For example, the bellwether process frequently educates the court regarding the merits of the claims which, in turn, may influence its approach to pre-trial motions. Likewise, because the same experts may be used in offering case-specific and generic opinions, to the extent those experts' opinions appear to be dubious in one area, it may influence the court regarding their opinions in other areas. For example, where an expert offers a flawed opinion regarding the cause of a particular plaintiff's alleged injury, that may influence the court in assessing the expert's opinions regarding whether a particular product is capable of causing injury more generally. Likewise, if an expert opines that a particular plaintiff's alleged injury was caused by a particular product and plaintiff counsel then seek to voluntarily dismiss the case, the court may well wonder about the credibility of the expert's opinions. Accordingly, the court's experience in one aspect of the MDL proceeding may inform its view of other aspects of the proceeding.

Parallel State Court Litigation

Another phenomenon that can undermine the successful resolution of multidistrict litigation is the existence of parallel state court litigation. As noted previously, the MDL statute does not provide a complete centralization of litigation—nor could it. Consistent with our federal system in which we have both state and federal courts that function in parallel, there may be litigation that is filed in state court and remains in state court despite the fact that a federal MDL proceeding has been established. As a result, there is a potential for significant litigation involving the same issues proceeding in parallel with the federal MDL. This state litigation may be widely dispersed, with individual cases filed before different judges in several different states, or it may be relatively consolidated with certain clusters of cases filed before the same state court judge or judges.

Indeed, many states have established rules that would provide not merely for the parallel litigation of individual cases, but the establishment of consolidated proceedings in state court similar to an MDL proceeding: "States increasingly have adopted procedures for assigning complex multiparty litigation to a single judge or judicial panel or have created courts to deal with complex business cases."[227] In some ways, this sort of state consolidation makes the task of coordination easier because the number of state court judges with which the MDL court must coordinate is reduced. However, in other ways, it may make things more difficult. Where a state court judge is presiding over a consolidated proceeding similar to an MDL proceeding involving numerous cases, that judge might feel that the state court should not defer to the federal MDL judge because the state court proceeding is of equal importance.

The existence of significant parallel state court proceedings can present the potential for significant problems and the erosion of some of the benefits the MDL procedures seek to obtain. First, and most obviously, absent coordination between state and federal courts, there is the potential for duplicative and inefficient discovery between the parallel proceedings. Documents may be produced multiple times, and the parties may seek to depose many of the same witnesses in both the federal MDL and the parallel state proceedings. As a result, at a minimum, there is the potential that efficiency may be reduced.

More concerning, absent coordination between federal and state court proceedings, there is the potential for parallel state proceedings to significantly interfere with the MDL proceeding. The state courts may impose obligations that are inconsistent with the federal proceedings. They may schedule trials that impair the smooth functioning of the MDL proceeding. For example, state courts may push forward with trials when the federal MDL court wants to give thorough attention to threshold legal or factual issues through pre-trial motion practice. This may have happened to some extent with respect to the litigation over the weed killer Roundup. In that litigation, state court trials occurred before the federal court had an opportunity to hold bellwether trials and when the federal court was in the middle of proceedings designed to assess the reliability of scientific evidence plaintiffs had submitted in support of their claim that Roundup was associated with cancer.

In fact, sometimes plaintiff counsel bring parallel state court litigation precisely for this reason. Plaintiff law firms that are denied a significant role in the federal MDL proceeding may then seek to pursue their claims in state court, where they can exercise more control over the litigation. They may attempt to push forward with the state court litigation in a manner that is contrary to the wishes of defendants, the MDL court, and their fellow plaintiff counsel.

Where an MDL fails to engage adequately, these problems may be magnified. State court judges may step into a vacuum left by an MDL judge who fails to make progress toward resolution. As a result, any coordination between the federal MDL and parallel state court litigation may break down. Where the MDL fails to progress, state court litigation may get out in front of the federal MDL and set the tone for the litigation.

Ultimately, the remedies for this sort of problem are not necessarily clear-cut, but there are a few things the MDL court can do to mitigate the problem. The MDL court can reach out to state court judges and attempt to coordinate proceedings with them, which is frequently a successful strategy. Independent guidelines, including the Federal Judicial Center's *Manual for Complex Litigation*, recommend such practices: "Effective coordination between the federal and state courts in an MDL action promotes cooperation in scheduling hearings, conducting and completing discovery, facilitates efficient distribution of and access to discovery work product, avoids inconsistent federal and state rulings on discovery and privilege issues, if possible, and fosters communication and cooperation among litigants and courts that may facilitate just and inexpensive determination."[228]

Whether they are members of the federal or state judiciary, judges typically recognize the value of coordination. Despite this recognition, there are occasions when state court judges may feel there is no need to coordinate with the federal MDL. Thus, for example, one recent article reported the results of interviews of state court judges regarding federal–state coordination that showed some state court judges had concerns about the process: "Some of the state court judges interviewed complained that MDLs have become more attractive than some class actions in state court, and that plaintiffs are using MDLs to 'jump around' the state court system."[229]

State courts traditionally handle the sorts of cases that are consolidated in large mass tort MDLs. Tort law is a creature of state law, and state courts are very familiar with such cases. They may question why they should defer to a federal MDL court, particularly when that court does not seem to be making progress in the litigation. Nonetheless, many overworked state courts may also be more than happy to let the federal court take the lead in resolving the litigation.

Accordingly, the extent of coordination in which state and federal judges are willing to engage may vary. The particular methods used to achieve coordination may vary as well: "Coordination may take many forms, and may vary in scope and degree depending on the needs of the cases and the interests of the state court judges. . . . Coordination methods include arrangements made by counsel, communications between judges, joint pretrial conferences and hearings at which all involved judges preside, and parallel orders."[230]

One trend in recent years is for the MDL court to issue an order specifically addressing coordination between the federal court and parallel state court proceedings. Some of the provisions courts may incorporate in such orders include creating joint federal–state plaintiff and defendant document depositories that are accessible to attorneys in all states, coordinating discovery between state courts and the federal MDL court to eliminate duplication, coordinating document production and arrangements for electronic discovery, ordering discovery materials from prior state and federal cases to be included in the document depository, scheduling and cross-noticing joint federal–state depositions, designating state-conducted depositions as official MDL depositions, and coordinating rulings on discovery disputes, such as the assertion of privilege, and using parallel or joint orders governing matters such as the preservation of evidence.[231]

The order Judge Furman issued in the *General Motors LLC Ignition Switch* litigation is illustrative. The court's order contained detailed provisions governing the coordination of discovery in the federal proceedings and coordinated state court proceedings. State courts presiding over parallel proceedings could elect to join the MDL court's order to authorize counsel in the state proceedings to join in coordinated discovery.[232] The order sought to coordinate discovery between the federal and state proceedings "to the fullest extent possible" by creating a single electronic document depository, granting access to discovery produced in the MDL to state counsel, providing for participation of state counsel in depositions taken in the MDL, and authorizing state counsel to apply for compensation from the common benefit fund.[233] Such formal coordination orders may become increasingly standard in large MDLs with significant parallel state court litigation.

In some MDLs, courts have endeavored to hold joint hearings with state court judges on topics such as the reliability of scientific evidence.[234] This occurred, for example, in the *PPA* cases in which the federal MDL court ended up granting *Daubert* motions that significantly narrowed the scope of the litigation. However, it is not particularly common, and probably less common today than it has been in the past. Discovery is another area that is "quite amenable to effective coordination" and may include "[t]he use of common experts, along with consolidated expert disclosures and expert discovery . . . ."[235] However, this level of coordination is not typical in MDL proceedings. It is difficult to achieve such a high level of coordination where there may be separate counsel in the state proceedings who wish to pursue their own strategies in litigating the cases and may want to retain their own expert witnesses.

Rather, in most proceedings, judges seek to communicate informally to make sure they do not interfere with the parallel proceedings. For example, the Federal Judicial Center recommends that MDL judges "reach out to [their] state court colleagues from the outset."[236] This may be accompanied by mechanisms designed to ensure that the MDL judge remains fully informed by requiring, for example, that the parties include updates on parallel state court proceedings in routine status reports to the court. In some cases, however, informal coordination efforts may fail, where, for example, state court judges are not interested in coordination or there is a significant and dispersed level of state court litigation in parallel with the federal MDL proceeding.

Another potential measure some courts employ is to use the power the court wields over lawyers who are in front of it to enforce some measure of coordination with state court proceedings. In some cases, lawyers representing clients in the state court litigation also represent clients in the federal court MDL. When this occurs, the court may utilize its influence with these lawyers to attempt to have them resolve potential conflicts that could arise between state court litigation and the federal MDL. The presence of the same lawyers in both jurisdictions may be an important factor in encouraging smooth coordination between the federal and state proceedings. However, in practice, lawyers on the plaintiffs' side tend to pick either state or federal court to pursue their cases. It may be only in instances where defendants are successful in removing cases to federal court that plaintiff counsel in the state court proceedings end up representing clients in the federal proceedings as well.

Another related measure the MDL court might employ is to designate a state court liaison who can attempt to facilitate coordination with state court proceedings. This state court liaison frequently is one of the plaintiff counsel in the MDL proceeding, or a committee of plaintiff counsel. Such individuals can use at least peer pressure to attempt to work with lawyers representing plaintiffs in the state court proceedings. They are then responsible to the MDL court presiding over the federal cases: "[E]xperienced transferee judges who have managed MDLs with and without state court liaisons have reported that they find that the appointment of a state court liaison greatly improves the MDL process, particularly in complex MDLs with a variety of state court matters."[237]

In addition, some courts have utilized special masters to coordinate between federal and state court proceedings through joint appointments: "Transferee judges that have used joint appointments report that it can be incredibly helpful in ensuring that discovery proceeds smoothly, but note that it takes the right case, right parties, and right situation for a joint appointment to be feasible."[238] One downside of this approach is the cost associated with the appointment of a special master. Moreover, typically matters such as the coordination of discovery can be accomplished without the need for such an appointment.

Finally, one other mechanism the MDL court can use to attempt to limit the effect of state court proceedings indirectly is to defer ruling on motions to remand cases back to state court that have been removed to federal court. When an MDL proceeding is established, defendants frequently attempt to channel as much of the litigation as they can to the MDL proceeding in federal court. As cases are filed in state court, defendants remove them to the federal districts in which the state courts are located. There is then frequently a race between plaintiffs and defendants, with plaintiffs seeking to have the federal court remand the case back to the state court while the defendants simultaneously ask the JPML to transfer the case to the MDL. As a general rule, the federal district courts that receive these cases tend to stay remand motions or defer ruling on them so the cases can be transferred to the MDL and the MDL court can then rule on the remand motions in the first instance. Accordingly, the MDL court typically has a population of cases that were originally in state court and must decide whether they should go back to state court or remain in the federal MDL proceedings.

Similarly, "[a]necdotes exist about transferee judges that have attempted to pressure plaintiffs' counsel into moving their cases into federal court, into the MDL."[239] The MDL court can attempt to encourage lawyers before the court to centralize cases within the federal MDL. In many instances, the lawyers will want to do so anyway and may not need much encouragement. However, ultimately, plaintiffs are free to choose where they file their cases, and the court has no power to do anything to prevent them from doing so.

Courts presiding over MDL proceedings often decide to defer ruling on such remand motions.[240] By doing so, they can avoid doing work that may not be necessary in the event the litigation is resolved or there is a settlement. However, such deferrals also have the effect of maximizing the number of cases in federal court and minimizing the number pending in state court. As a result, courts employing such procedures minimize the chances that state court litigation will disrupt the MDL proceedings.

Dissatisfaction with the Sole Decision Maker

As noted previously, one of the complaints surrounding MDL proceedings involves the selection of judges that the parties view as being outliers who may favor one side or the other in the MDL proceeding. However, even where the parties may be content with the initial selection, based on the judge's management of the MDL and the judge's rulings, they may become dissatisfied. Given current practices, there are only limited mechanisms available to the parties to attempt to ameliorate this situation.

Judges presiding over an MDL have significant power over the course of the proceeding. The efficiencies obtained by sending the litigation to a single decision maker are inherently bound up with the potential that one side or the other will become dissatisfied with that single decision maker as the MDL progresses. A single decision maker is a great advantage if that decision maker is consistently ruling in your favor, but not so much if the rulings are consistently against you.

As noted in prior chapters, some MDL courts have employed third parties to assist them in their work, which may to some minor extent mitigate this risk. Magistrates or special masters may assist the court in its rulings with respect to discovery or other matters. Moreover, although they have rarely done so in MDL proceedings, federal judges may also select their own independent experts to provide input on critical issues in the proceedings. Decades ago, the MDL court presiding over litigation alleging that breast implants caused a variety of diseases did so, empaneling a body of independent experts who concluded that there was no reliable scientific evidence demonstrating that breast implants were associated with disease. More recently, MDL courts have employed experts in electronic discovery to assist them in making rulings with respect to discovery disputes. However, as noted, while MDL courts have appointed special masters and magistrates to some extent, they have not commonly appointed independent experts. Parties frequently are against the use of independent experts because it reduces their ability to control the direction of the litigation and introduces an element of uncertainty into the proceedings.

Another tactic that, somewhat surprisingly, has not been more regularly employed in MDL proceedings is the use of interlocutory appeal to attempt to obtain review by appellate courts of the MDL judge's key rulings during the course of the proceedings. Under federal law, the general rule is that parties in litigation may not appeal until there is a final ruling at the end of the proceedings. This allows the appellate court to consider all issues in a case at once, which is frequently more efficient. However, in some cases it is more efficient for the appellate court to consider important issues that may arise during the course of a case. For example, the federal rules seek to facilitate appellate review of trial court decisions concerning whether to certify a class action.[241] The decision regarding whether to certify a class is a significant decision that can affect how the case is litigated going forward. Whether a single plaintiff is at issue compared to an entire class of individuals can impact the proceedings significantly. Accordingly, the rules implicitly recognize that facilitating appellate review of such a decision in the middle of a proceeding increases the efficiency of the litigation, given the importance of the decision and the number of claims that it potentially impacts.

More generally, federal law provides the possibility of obtaining interlocutory appellate review of important decisions that arise during the course of litigation.[242] However, it imposes some potential barriers to doing so. Generally, to obtain appellate review of a decision in the middle of a case under 28 U.S.C. § 1292(b), the party seeking such review must obtain the permission of both the trial court and the appellate court. If either court denies the request for interlocutory review, then none will occur. Accordingly, the barriers to obtaining interlocutory review can be significant.

Nonetheless, as the Federal Judicial Center has observed, "[m]any judges use the interlocutory appeal procedure afforded by 28 U.S.C. § 1292(b) to allow appellate review of critical rulings while other aspects of the case move forward."[243] Indeed, "[s]ome legal issues may be susceptible to resolution and review on interlocutory appeal relatively early in the litigation. Examples include whether claims are cognizable under federal common law, barred by the statute of limitations, subject to issue or claim preclusion, or covered by insurance."[244]

In the context of an MDL proceeding where there are potentially thousands of cases at issue, arguably the case for interlocutory review is even stronger. With respect to key rulings on motions for summary judgment or motions to dismiss that may be dispositive with respect to many of the cases, it frequently is more efficient to obtain appellate input in the middle of a proceeding. If an MDL court denies such dispositive motions when the appellate court would hold that they should be granted, the parties may incur a huge amount of time and expense needlessly. Such dispositive motions shape the scope of the subsequent litigation, and where thousands of cases are at issue in an MDL proceeding it may be more efficient to resolve those issues through the appellate stage as quickly as possible.

Moreover, there are aspects of an MDL proceeding that may make it unlikely that there ever will be appellate review of important decisions absent some form of interlocutory review. Where an MDL proceeding follows the settlement model, there may never be any appellate review. Defendants may be pressured to enter into a global settlement of all claims before there is any final judgment and any opportunity to seek appellate review as a matter of right. In addition, where a defendant consistently obtains defense verdicts in bellwether trials, there may be no opportunity for appellate review, given that the defendant has no basis to appeal from trials in which it prevailed on all issues. In other words, it is possible that defendants consistently prevail when the claims are subject to scrutiny either in trial or through pre-trial motions and, as a result, the defendant never has a right to take an appeal of any of the trial court's decisions.

In any event, it is almost certain that any opportunity for review as a matter of right after final judgment will occur only after the defendants have litigated in the MDL proceeding for a significant period of time. Where, as in a large MDL proceeding, there are hundreds or thousands of claims at issue, it simply takes time before the court begins issuing final rulings that provide an opportunity for appellate review.

Despite the potential benefits, a survey of appeals from MDL cases shows that interlocutory review is relatively rare. Most appeals arising out of MDL proceedings involve final orders that are appealable as of right. A recent survey concluded: "Almost all of these cases made it up on appeal via § 1291, typically appealing a grant of dismissal, summary judgment, an order for fees, or under Rule 23(f) as appeals of class certification decisions. There were a handful of interlocutory appeals via 28 U.S.C. § 1292 and one mandamus."[245]

Such interlocutory review is not uncommon in other similar proceedings. In large Chapter 11 bankruptcy proceedings that involve mass tort claims, for example, it is not unusual for the bankruptcy court's rulings to be reviewed on an interlocutory basis.[246] In the context of bankruptcy proceedings there may be two levels of appellate review. Both the district court presiding over the bankruptcy and then the appellate court may review a bankruptcy court's interlocutory orders. Such review is more frequent in the context of large bankruptcy proceedings, and yet the issues may be similar, given that both MDL and bankruptcy courts presiding over large numbers of mass tort claims may be required to address similar issues regarding causation and other matters. Similarly, interlocutory review has occurred in state court proceedings where numerous claims have been consolidated before a single judge.

A shift in the attitude of MDL and appellate courts may therefore be warranted. If courts became more comfortable with interlocutory appeal in the context of an MDL proceeding, it might make such proceedings more efficient by giving guidance to the MDL court during the course of the proceedings. MDLs typically last years, and thus there is certainly time to seek appellate review. Moreover, the proceedings need not be stayed completely while the appellate court reviews the MDL court's rulings. Progress can be made while appeals are pending.

There already appears to be some movement in this regard. In certain large MDL proceedings, the parties have sought to obtain appellate review of the MDL court's decisions on an interlocutory basis. Where the parties have been unable to obtain the MDL court's consent to an interlocutory appeal under Section 1292(b), they have sought to have the appellate court review the MDL court's actions by pursuing a writ of mandamus. In the *National Prescription Opiate* litigation, for example, parties have filed more than one petition for a writ of mandamus challenging a number of the MDL court's rulings, including the MDL judge's refusal to recuse himself and rulings on discovery matters.[247]

While mandamus is an extraordinary remedy and not routinely granted, in the *Opiate* litigation the Sixth Circuit granted a petition for mandamus after concluding that the MDL court's orders either "disregarded" or were "in flat contradiction to" the rules of civil procedure.[248] Several pharmacies that had been sued in the litigation filed the petition, alleging that the MDL court erred by allowing plaintiffs to amend their complaints to add claims against them as dispensers of prescription opioids after the deadline had passed, allowing wide-ranging discovery on the newly filed claims, including requests for nearly every opioid prescription the defendant pharmacies had filed anywhere in the United States for the past 13 years, and then refusing to rule on the defendant pharmacies' motions to dismiss the claims on the ground that the court had barred defendants from making "*any* non-jurisdictional motions to dismiss."[249] The court of appeals ruled the MDL court should not have allowed the plaintiffs to amend their complaints long after the deadline for amendment contained in the MDL court's scheduling order had passed.

As the appellate court observed, allowing the amendment was at odds with Rule 16(b), which required that scheduling orders "must limit the time" for amending the pleadings and that leave to amend could not be granted absent a showing that the party had put forth at least a diligent effort to comply with the court's deadline.[250] The appellate court concluded that the plaintiffs could not make such a showing. It noted that the plaintiffs had not only failed to bring their claims by the court's deadline, but "they *expressly chose not to bring them*," which the appellate court concluded "arguably amounts to an outright waiver of them."[251] Moreover, while the appellate court concluded that the other issues the pharmacy defendants raised were moot because plaintiffs should not have been allowed to amend their complaints in the first place, it further observed that the MDL court could not simply "refuse to adjudicate motions properly filed under" Rule 12(b)(6).[252] It therefore granted the petition.

In the process of issuing this ruling, the appellate court underscored that, "[t]he rule of law applies in multidistrict litigation under 28 U.S.C. § 1407 just as it does in any individual case."[253] As it observed, "MDLs are not some kind of judicial border country, where the rules are few and the law rarely makes an appearance."[254] The appellate court thus pushed back on the notion that MDLs had some special status in which the normal rules governing litigants in federal court might be relaxed in the interest of "enhancing the efficiency of the MDL as a whole."[255] Rather, the court observed that, "the law governs an MDL court's decisions just as it does a court's decisions in any other case."[256]

Such decisions may portend a greater use of mandamus as a mechanism for obtaining review of interlocutory MDL court rulings. As with an interlocutory appeal under Section 1292(b), the fact that review is sought from an order issued in an MDL proceeding is a factor that arguably supports review of a petition for mandamus. Courts typically recognize that mandamus is "particularly appropriate" where the issue that is the subject of the petition has importance "beyond the immediate case."[257] This would be true of many issues arising in an MDL proceeding involving potentially hundreds or thousands of cases.

Thus, in the future, interlocutory review may become more common in MDL proceedings. A culture that is more accepting of interlocutory review may develop among the parties and the courts involved in MDLs, leading to a greater number of orders granting review under Section 1292(b). The development of such a culture would provide a check on the possibility that outlier rulings may skew the proceedings. Nonetheless, under the current framework, the parties would still have to obtain the approval of the MDL judge to obtain interlocutory review.

Dissatisfaction with the Jury Pool

The jury pool in the MDL jurisdiction may also be a concern. There are differences across the United States in terms of the propensity of juries to award significant damages in the sorts of cases typically centralized in an MDL proceeding. In some jurisdictions, juries may award billion-dollar verdicts in individual cases. In other jurisdictions, there may be defense verdicts in comparable cases or the damages may be much smaller. Accordingly, where bellwether trials are part of MDL proceedings, there can be a great diversity in potential outcomes depending on the jurisdiction in which an MDL is established.

One procedure that may provide some remedy to this problem is for the MDL court to send certain bellwethers to other jurisdictions for trial. While not particularly common in MDL proceedings, the MDL court has the power to remand individual cases for trial in the courts from which they were transferred. Accordingly, an MDL court could employ an approach to bellwether trials that involved trying individual cases in separate jurisdictions around the country to get a more diverse set of results from different jury pools.

Even where the MDL court does not remand cases to other jurisdictions, there may be cases pending in other jurisdictions already that were not centralized as part of the MDL proceedings that could be scheduled for trial while the MDL is pending. Whether intentional or not, this scenario is more common. Because an MDL proceeding may not completely centralize litigation, there are frequently parallel proceedings in state courts that can result in trials either before or after bellwether trials in the MDL proceeding begin. Accordingly, it is not uncommon to have trial results from multiple jurisdictions regardless of the procedures in the MDL proceeding.

As noted, state court trials can disrupt the MDL process; however, they can also provide information regarding the value of the claims. They may also provide a vehicle for achieving some measure of diversity in terms of trial results. However, the state court jurisdictions in which cases are filed are usually carefully selected by plaintiff counsel. Accordingly, these results may prove to be skewed as well. The results may be due to forum-shopping, leading to trial outcomes that are biased in favor of plaintiffs. In any event, the availability of state court proceedings provides another potential source of information to assess the value of claims filed in the litigation, completely independent of the federal MDL proceeding.

Problems with Settlement Administration

Finally, even where the parties reach a consensual settlement, there can be significant problems. As can be expected, whenever there is a large amount of money at stake, there is an incentive to cut corners or engage in outright fraud. If the criteria for determining which plaintiffs should receive payment and the amount they should receive are not rigorous or clear enough under the settlement agreement, there can be substantial payments to those who should not receive them. This may potentially disadvantage plaintiffs who have more meritorious claims as settlement funds are depleted.

Indeed, there have been a number of instances in which there were public accusations of fraud in the administration of large MDL settlements. The *NFL Concussion* MDL provides one example. That litigation involved claims brought by former football players who alleged that they had unnecessarily suffered concussions while playing for the National Football League. As Professor Burch recounts in her book, "the NFL claimed that 'widespread fraud' infected the settlement program and asked Judge Brody to appoint a special investigator. It alleged that players' lawyers coached them on how to answer neuropsychological exams, sent them to pediatric neurologists, and submitted reports that included identical vital signs for 21 different players."[258] The court ended up dismissing three out of four of the class counsel representing plaintiffs in the settlement class that the court had certified.

Defendants in the *Deepwater Horizon* MDL alleged that there was similar fraudulent conduct with respect to the settlement fund established to pay claimants after the Deepwater Horizon oil spill in the Gulf of Mexico. There, BP and claimants' counsel negotiated a settlement agreement that provided significant compensation for individuals who alleged they suffered economic damages as the result of the oil spill. However, once the settlement fund began issuing payments, it quickly appeared that many of the claims that had been submitted lacked merit. Based on its review, BP estimated that the settlement fund was paying up to $100 million per week in fraudulent claims. To publicize the fraud, the company took out full-page advertisements in newspapers, decrying what it described as outrageous claims. Ultimately, the Department of Justice prosecuted and convicted hundreds of individuals for defrauding the settlement fund.[259]

In some ways, these examples should be no surprise. The same dynamics that cause plaintiffs to file meritless claims in an MDL proceeding lead to meritless claims at the settlement stage. However, claims administrators responsible for making payments under a settlement agreement may be even less rigorous than an MDL court in reviewing the claims. The process is more of an administrative one than an adversarial one, with little incentive for rigorous scrutiny of asserted claims.

Indeed, there is a long history of problems in the administration of large funds responsible for making payments to tort claimants.[260] For example, there has long been a concern that trusts established to pay asbestos-related tort claims brought against companies that went into bankruptcy have been paying claims that are fraudulent. There is at least anecdotal evidence that claimants have made inconsistent representations regarding the asbestos-containing products to which they were exposed to maximize their recoveries against multiple defendants. In the court system or when filing a claim with one asbestos trust, plaintiffs may claim exposure to one set of products to receive compensation while denying or failing to mention such exposure when subsequently filing a claim against another trust. Because there is little transparency with respect to the claims-filing process and these filings are not always public, it is possible that many meritless claims are receiving compensation from multiple sources.

10
Proposals for Reform

As discussed in the preceding chapters, federal courts presiding over MDL proceedings have a number of tools available to them under the current rules that, if employed effectively, allow them to resolve MDL proceedings in an efficient manner. Nonetheless, as also noted, courts have not always employed these tools in an effective manner, and dissatisfaction with MDL practice continues to grow. This dissatisfaction, in turn, has resulted in proposals for reform of the governing rules and statutes.[261] However, this dissatisfaction has also led to significant efforts to develop guidelines or best practices, such as those promulgated by Duke Law School's Bolch Judicial Institute, to improve MDL practice using the existing rules and procedures.

The extent to which reforms are implemented remains to be seen. There is an ongoing debate regarding which formal reforms would be appropriate and the extent to which they should be applied to multidistrict litigation. Within the broad category of multidistrict litigation, there can be a significant diversity of cases. An MDL court may preside over litigation as varied as antitrust and product liability claims. There are massive MDLs involving thousands of claims and smaller MDLs involving only a few cases. There are MDLs in which the cases involve many diverse factual issues and MDLs that involve primarily common legal issues. Moreover, some have expressed the view that "the problems seemed to be concentrated in the 'mega-MDLs' that aggregate thousands and tens of thousands of cases."[262] As a result, some have suggested that a one-size-fits-all approach may not be the most appropriate for reform of MDL cases. However, others have argued that MDL procedures should be general in nature and there is a broad-based need for reform.

In addition, there has been a debate regarding the proper role of the judge in an MDL proceeding. Some judges view their role in an MDL proceeding as a flexible one, and have expressed reservations regarding efforts to require that certain procedures be employed in every case. They view their role as developing procedures to fit the case. Accordingly, there can be resistance to constraining the freedom of MDL judges to craft procedures to match the unique circumstances of each case. However, such concerns often run up against the broad-based consensus that there are significant problems that have occurred in MDL cases that need to be addressed and the view that the discretion of judges in MDL cases must be more constrained.

Finally, even among those who advocate for formal reform efforts, there has been a debate with respect to specific proposals. There are so many stakeholders involved in MDL proceedings with so many disparate interests that it can be difficult to reach consensus. However, these diverse views have led to an equal diversity in the proposals for reform of the system, with many commentators suggesting creative proposals that have the potential to improve the efficiency and fairness of MDL proceedings in significant ways.

Because of these and other factors, the outcome of these reform efforts remains to be seen. As the Civil Rules Advisory Committee has observed, "[t]here seems to be some measure of agreement that there is a problem with unfounded individual cases, but not so much agreement on the prospect of finding a solution in a court rule."[263] Nonetheless, it may be that in the future, reform of MDL procedures will address some of the problems all agree exist in MDL proceedings.

Even if complete reform of the system does not occur, however, the process itself can still have significant benefits. The reforms that have been proposed identify aspects of the system that participants view as problematic. They are targeted at certain areas in which the critics of MDL procedure believe there are flaws in the system. As with many reform efforts, even where formal reforms of rules or statutes ultimately are not implemented, the reform movement itself may result in the adoption of improved procedures that can be implemented under the current rules. Indeed, as we will see, to some extent the proposed rule and statutory changes seem to be aimed at codifying procedures that MDL judges have already employed successfully to resolve MDL proceedings. Nonetheless, there are also aspects of the proposed reforms that can only be accomplished through formal changes to the existing rules and statutes.

Initial Disclosures

One example of a proposed reform that seems to mirror established procedures can be found in draft legislation pending before Congress entitled the *Fairness in Class Action Litigation Act of 2017*. The bill would codify initial disclosure requirements by requiring that plaintiffs provide evidence of their alleged injury within 45 days of transfer to the MDL proceeding.[264] The judge would then be required to promptly determine the sufficiency of each plaintiff submission and dismiss without prejudice those submissions that are insufficient. If the deficiency is not cured, the court would then dismiss the claim with prejudice.

These proposed requirements are similar to procedures MDL courts frequently employ. As noted, it is standard practice for MDL courts to require plaintiffs to fill out fact sheets that contain information such as the alleged injury the plaintiff suffered and information regarding product identification. The proposed reforms would go further in the sense that they would require plaintiffs to take the additional step of pointing to the evidence that supports their claims. In doing so, the reforms would shift the cost to some extent to the plaintiffs. Instead of having defendants look through the evidence to refute plaintiffs' allegations, the proposed reforms would have plaintiffs do the initial work of identifying the evidence that supports their claims. As the legislation observes, its purpose is to "diminish abuses in class action and mass tort litigation that are undermining the integrity of the U.S. legal system."[265]

Such reforms are similar to the administrative orders some courts have issued that require plaintiffs to identify the documents that demonstrate they have an injury and actually were exposed to the product that allegedly caused their injury. The proposed reforms would move toward making such procedures mandatory. The problem these orders seek to remedy is the large number of claims that have been filed in MDL proceedings, apparently with little investigation, which turn out to be unsupported. Lawyers have an ethical obligation to investigate claims to make sure they are supportable before they file them. However, the large volume of claims filed and the active recruiting of plaintiffs through advertising may result in ineffective screening. The reforms would ensure that such screening occurs at the beginning of the proceedings and largely place the cost and burden of that screening on plaintiff counsel.

Another proposal relating to early disclosure has been raised before the Advisory Committee on Rules of Civil Procedure. The proposal would consider whether there is a need for some sort of more streamlined review at the outset of the proceedings, dubbed an "initial census." Such a procedure would again provide a potential means of eliminating claims that are obviously flawed, much like review of plaintiff fact sheets. However, less information would be required, and the burden of providing the information would be on the plaintiffs bringing the claims. In particular, the census in a product liability case would require that plaintiffs collect information sufficient to establish a *prima facie* case with respect to issues such as "exposure and injury."[266]

However, from the defendants' perspective, there may be a potential danger in such proposals in that, if not implemented correctly, they could threaten to further reduce the information plaintiffs provide at the outset of an MDL, allowing flawed claims to escape scrutiny. There is already a potential danger that plaintiff fact sheets supplant the normal procedures for discovery available to litigants in civil cases filed in federal court. The census proposal might have the unintended consequence of exacerbating this situation, to the extent courts believe plaintiff fact sheets are no longer necessary where a census has occurred.

While there are certainly costs associated with defense review of plaintiff fact sheets, and the fact sheets frequently are incomplete or contain information that is inaccurate, the documents produced with the fact sheets or in conjunction with authorizations provided with the fact sheets usually are extremely useful. They allow defendants and the court to apply at least some level of scrutiny to the claims. A "census" as defined by the proponents of this proposal would by definition be more streamlined and contain less information and, therefore, would inherently be less valuable. Defendants may be left holding the bag in the event that whatever disclosures are required by the census are so flawed or cursory that they do not allow any progress to be made in the litigation. Accordingly, in the event that a census is implemented, it should be used to supplement, rather than displace, other procedures for information gathering. Courts must ensure that the parties have basic information necessary to evaluate the claims as early as possible in the MDL proceedings; otherwise, it will be impossible to weed out claims that should not have been filed.

In addition to potential deficiencies in the factual disclosures plaintiffs make early in a case, an even more significant issue may be the degree to which the parties and the court utilize that information to eliminate meritless claims. There are many ways in which MDL courts presiding over large-scale MDL cases have required plaintiffs to produce certain basic information early in the proceedings. While none of these mechanisms may be perfect, at least some fundamental information generally is provided. To the extent there are failures in screening cases filed in MDLs, the failure frequently seems to be located at the subsequent stage in which information is reviewed and the court is called on to take action to eliminate claims that are unsupported or otherwise lack merit. Courts may fail in this screening process or may fail to attend to it early in the proceedings. This delay can be the fault of the parties where they fail to promptly review the information and, where necessary, seek relief from the court. However, it may also be the fault of MDL courts that fail to promptly eliminate claims that on their face are meritless based on the information provided.

The reform proposals also attempt to address this aspect of the problem. Proposals such as the *Fairness in Class Action Litigation Act*, for example, would require MDL courts to take certain action at the outset of the proceedings. The proposed Act would require that plaintiffs provide the initial disclosure of information within 45 days and then, 90 days after that deadline, the MDL court would determine whether the submission is sufficient. The court would dismiss the action initially without prejudice if the submission were insufficient and would dismiss the case with prejudice within 30 days after that if the deficiency were not cured.[267]

However, beyond merely reviewing the sufficiency of such initial submissions, it may be difficult to require MDL courts by rule or statute to do the work necessary to review and rule on the actual merits of the claims based on the initial submissions. This is particularly true in our adversarial system, where it is up to the parties to make their arguments and courts take a comparatively passive role, ruling only on the issues that are before them that have been raised by the parties. Accordingly, even if such reforms were adopted, there could still be significant issues regarding review and assessment of obvious deficiencies in terms of the merits of the asserted claims. In any event, requiring plaintiffs to take even the most basic step of actually producing information to support their claims can result in the elimination of claims plaintiffs are unwilling to prosecute.

Interlocutory Appeals

Another proposed reform that appears to have some traction would be to facilitate interlocutory appellate review in MDL proceedings. Under the proposed *Fairness in Class Action Litigation Act*, parties would be entitled to interlocutory appeal of orders that "may materially advance the ultimate termination of one or more civil actions in the proceedings."[268] While the scope of this new proposed appellate right is not unlimited, but rather restricted to certain kinds of MDL court orders, it would provide more ready access to appellate review of the MDL court's most significant rulings.

As noted in the prior chapter, in the context of MDL proceedings the current interlocutory appeal statute receives relatively "infrequent use."[269] "The proponents of expanding interlocutory review emphasize that in MDL mass tort litigation defendants have found it difficult or impossible to obtain review of core legal issues such as preemption until after a bellwether trial, and perhaps not even then if defendants win at trial."[270] One of the potential barriers to more frequent use of interlocutory review is that the approval of both the MDL court and the appellate court is required to obtain it. Some have argued that language in the statute referencing controlling questions of law may also make courts hesitant to grant review of questions that involve significant questions of fact.

The MDL court may veto appellate review for a variety of reasons. It may feel its ruling was correct and appellate review would be a waste of time. It may feel appellate review would unnecessarily delay the proceedings, or it may simply believe there is not an overwhelming need for appellate review at that stage of the proceedings. In addition, even if the MDL court approves the request for appellate review, the court of appeals may reject it. Data collected in conjunction with discussions regarding MDL reforms before the Advisory Committee on Rules of Civil Procedure indicate that, "even when the district court has certified orders for immediate review, courts of appeals often decide not to take the appeals, as the statute permits."[271]

In some ways, this may be simply an illustration of a self-fulfilling prophecy. The relative rarity of interlocutory appeals arising out of MDL proceedings may lead either MDL courts or appellate courts to deny future requests. To the extent requests for interlocutory appeal were more common, courts might be more inclined to grant such requests. There would be a track record demonstrating that they provide a valuable procedural mechanism to improve, rather than detract from, the efficiency of MDL proceedings.

Plaintiff counsel would say that defendants have simply failed to request interlocutory review and this is the reason it is not more common in MDL proceedings. Nonetheless, the fact remains that under the current rules, it is a matter within the discretion of two different courts—the MDL court that issued the ruling that is the subject of review and the appellate court that reviews it. If either court declines to grant interlocutory review, it will be denied.

The proposed legislation would remedy this situation by making review of certain orders mandatory. Orders that are dispositive of the litigation would be subject to mandatory interlocutory review under this proposal. This reform would attempt to mitigate the possibility that outlier rulings in an MDL proceeding might put pressure on the parties to settle before any review of those rulings could be obtained from the appellate court. Under the current system, it is possible that a defendant could lose pre-trial motions, prevail in a bellwether trial, and not be able to obtain review of the pre-trial rulings until the defendant lost a bellwether trial and there was a final judgment against the defendant. Frequently in MDL proceedings, no appellate review is ever obtained because the cases never make it to the appellate court before they are settled. The proposed reforms seek to remedy this situation.

Plaintiffs counter that such reforms would be inefficient because they would require a separate proceeding in the middle of the MDL that could prolong the proceedings.[272] Moreover, they maintain that interlocutory review is currently available and the only reason it is not more common is that defendants do not request it more frequently. However, absent reform, there exists no certain path to appellate review on an interlocutory basis. Moreover, the nature of the proceedings is quite different from an individual case. Much like interlocutory review in the context of a mass tort bankruptcy or a class action proceeding, interlocutory review in the context of an MDL proceeding can provide guidance for hundreds or thousands of individual claims. The fact that an MDL involves multiple claims arguably provides an additional impetus to facilitating appellate review before a final order.

Commentators have suggested other reforms to facilitate interlocutory appellate review. Many of these proposals involve attempts to accelerate interlocutory review in the context of an MDL proceeding.[273] As a threshold matter, while some have argued that one downside of interlocutory appeal is the potential for delay, in fact, such concerns are probably lessened in an MDL proceeding. Given that there may be hundreds or thousands of claims pending before it, there is plenty for an MDL court to do while an interlocutory appeal is pending. Moreover, depending on the circumstances, there may be no need to stay the entire proceeding while the appeal is pending, and the court may use the time as it normally would to continue making progress in the litigation. Where, for example, the issue on appeal involves certain rulings on dispositive motions concerning common issues, the court can turn its attention to resolving case-specific issues or overseeing discovery in certain areas. In sum, interlocutory appellate review can be accommodated easily in the context of a large MDL proceeding.

Moreover, if there is a concern with delay in a particular MDL, the parties are not left without a remedy under the current rules. The parties can seek expedited resolution of the appeal before the court of appeals. The appellate court may well be receptive to such requests, given the large number of cases that are typically at issue in an MDL proceeding and the significance of those proceedings. Moreover, as requests for interlocutory review become more common in MDL proceedings, a culture may develop within the judiciary in which appellate courts understand the importance of expedited review in the context of an MDL proceeding. The use of such procedures itself might, in turn, eventually make them a more viable option as their use becomes more accepted by the federal judiciary.

Nonetheless, greater efficiency is certainly a desirable goal and, to the extent proposals for reform can accelerate the appellate process, they may be warranted. One possibility is simply to put appeals from MDL proceedings on an accelerated schedule that takes precedence over other pending appeals. Another proposal might be to establish review by some form of permanent panel that is familiar with the sorts of issues that arise in MDL proceedings.[274] In sum, there are a number of ways in which interlocutory appeal could be made even more efficient in the context of MDL proceedings.

Bellwether Trials

Another reform motivated by a skepticism regarding the bellwether process would preclude the trial of a claim in an MDL proceeding unless all parties consent to trial.[275] This reform would effectively provide each side with a veto over bellwether trials in the MDL. Already under the MDL statute and Supreme Court precedent, parties may object to the trial of cases that were transferred to the MDL court from other jurisdictions. As previously discussed, the Supreme Court in *Lexecon v. Milberg Weiss Bershad Hynes & Lerach* held that the parties could veto bellwether trials of cases originally filed in other courts and subsequently transferred to the MDL court.[276] Accordingly, at least with respect to a sizeable subset of the MDL case inventory, the parties theoretically have a veto on the trial of cases in the MDL.

However, there is significant pressure that the MDL court may bring to bear in an effort to get the parties to waive their *Lexecon* rights. As a result, "'*Lexecon* waivers,' where parties consent to trial in the transferee court, are increasingly common."[277] Absent such a waiver, bellwether trials may not be particularly representative. Excluding claims that were transferred to the MDL could potentially skew the results of the bellwether process. Yet, there have been instances in which both plaintiffs and defendants have refused to waive their *Lexecon* rights. Plaintiffs may file their cases in a jurisdiction they believe is more favorable than the jurisdiction selected for the MDL. Likewise, defendants may decide that the MDL court would be less favorable than the jurisdiction in which the cases were originally filed.

The proposed reform would extend the right to object to the trial of cases to all cases in an MDL proceeding. In this way, the reform would potentially cut back on the use of bellwethers in MDL proceedings. However, there would still be the potential that the MDL court could pressure the parties to waive their new statutory rights, in which case the potential impact of the proposed reform could be reduced. In any event, this reform again illustrates the problems that at least defendants perceive in the current way in which the MDL process functions. In addition to the problem of meritless claims and the potential for outlier decisions that are not subject to review, defendants view the bellwether process as potentially flawed and have sought changes that would improve the process.

Settlement

Another avenue for reform entertained by the Advisory Committee on Rules of Civil Procedure is whether there should be some rule governing the role of an MDL judge in settlement. Accordingly, the committee has considered whether the MDL judge should be required to review settlements the parties reach in MDL proceedings, somewhat similar to what occurs with respect to class action settlements under Rule 23. Given the potential concerns some have expressed with having judges involve themselves significantly in settlement, the committee has also considered whether there might be an independent entity that could review MDL settlements.

As the committee has explained, "[s]ettlement review has been urged on the ground that at least in the MDLs that include a great many cases settlement negotiations come to resemble class actions but without protective features built into Rule 23. The fear is that plaintiffs represented by lawyers who do not participate in the centralized steering committee structure are not afforded a genuine opportunity for meaningful individual settlement negotiations."[278]

Those who argue in favor of some formalized review note many of the same concerns discussed in prior chapters. Settlement in the context of an MDL proceeding is every bit as significant as settlement in the context of a class action. However, the procedural protections present under the class action rule are not always present under the MDL framework. Some have suggested that the issue of settlement is not addressed by statute or by rule in the context of MDL proceedings because those proceedings were originally intended to address pre-trial proceedings only, and there was no expectation that settlement would become as common as it has become in recent years. Moreover, unlike in the context of class actions under Rule 23, MDLs do not raise the problem of absent class members whose interests must be protected where there is a class-wide settlement that may bind them. Nonetheless, in an MDL proceeding, many of the plaintiffs in the litigation and their lawyers are along for the ride and have no significant ability to control the litigation. Accordingly, some have argued that at least some effort should be made to protect their interests with respect to a settlement that may determine the outcome of their claims.

A less rigid approach has been discussed before the Advisory Committee on Rules of Civil Procedure. The proposal would add a rule that would address the MDL court's authority to appoint leadership committees. The committee has indicated that such a rule "could be a way to introduce the desired judicial authority regarding MDL settlements into the civil rules."[279] However, it would do so in an indirect fashion, rather than expressly addressing the MDL court's role in settlement negotiations.

There is, however, a significant debate about whether, or how, this issue should be handled by rule. The problem here is a familiar one. Judges have different views about how involved the MDL court should be in the negotiation and approval of a settlement. There is a range of perspectives on whether active judicial involvement is appropriate or desirable. Moreover, if the same cases that are part of an MDL were remanded to the transferor courts, they would be subject to no such rule. Civil cases are settled every day in the federal system without the sort of review that reformers seem to contemplate in raising these proposals.

Moreover, it appears some participants in the MDL process are opposed to having a formal rule that would involve the court in settlement in some pre-defined way. As the Advisory Committee recently reported: "Thus far it appears that the lawyers we have heard from oppose rules authorizing judicial involvement in the settlement process. And it seems that most transferee judges do not want such rules, and do not think they need them."[280] However, as the committee further noted, the lawyers involved in the rules amendment process are primarily those who benefit from the current system, which provides significant financial rewards for those in leadership positions: "Given that we have heard mainly from MDL 'insiders,' and given the likelihood that some 'outsiders' (the lawyers who find a portion of their fees assigned to a common benefit fund and paid to 'insider' lawyers in leadership positions) could resist any such rules, caution is in order."[281]

Other Reforms

Finally, some have proposed even more creative reforms of the MDL system. For example, one proposal would break up large MDLs among multiple judges to address the perceived problem with having a single decision maker preside over such a large litigation without effective means of obtaining interlocutory review.[282] However, as an MDL is divided, the potential for efficiency may be reduced as the judges presiding over the MDL must coordinate with each other and there is the potential for duplicative proceedings. The question is whether the potential costs of such a proposal outweigh the benefits. In any event, such proposals illustrate the extent to which there is dissatisfaction with the current MDL system.

The more fundamental question is the degree to which progress may be made in the absence of formal rule changes. Those who support the current system, primarily those in the plaintiff's bar, would argue that it has resolved literally hundreds of thousands of cases. Their view may be akin to "if it ain't broke, don't fix it." While some in the plaintiff's bar maintain there is no problem with meritless claims flooding the system, many acknowledge that, at least to some extent, there is a failure in screening out weak claims. However, regardless of their views on whether there is a problem, they are relatively committed to the current system from which they have significantly profited and are leery of any major change.

Others maintain that while there have been problems in the MDL system, to some extent they can be addressed using the current rules. As illustrated in the prior chapters, there are many examples where MDL courts have utilized the current framework effectively to resolve large-scale MDL proceedings in a just and efficient manner. Courts have employed a variety of procedures to weed out claims on an individual basis. They have acted decisively in granting generic motions where appropriate. And there are procedures available by which parties may seek interlocutory review of MDL court rulings, at least on a discretionary basis. Therefore, in many instances the current rules may be used to beneficial effect. Nonetheless, for every such example involving a successful resolution, critics of the MDL system can point to multiple examples where the system has failed.

In addition, some have expressed a concern that to some extent reforms may tie the hands of judges in MDL proceedings who may want to exercise a greater degree of flexibility in resolving the litigation. For example, some have argued that a one-size-fits-all initial disclosure regime may not be the most efficient approach to all MDL cases. One could well imagine that there are some MDL cases where the court will want to address common or generic issues first. For example, the court in the *Incretin Mimetics* MDL came to just such a conclusion, determining that there were significant questions regarding whether the pharmaceuticals at issue were associated with pancreatic cancer. As noted, the FDA had looked at the question and concluded that there was no causal association and, indeed, had issued public notices to that effect stating that no additional warnings were necessary in the labeling for these products. Indeed, the FDA expressed concern that such allegations could cause patients to discontinue their medications based on a fear that they may develop cancer, causing them significant harm. Given this record, the federal court presiding over the MDL quickly established a schedule to tee up these issues at the outset of the proceedings.[283] The court stated that it would address defendants' argument that the FDA action preempted plaintiffs' claims and then would move on, if necessary, to decide generic causation. Arguably, spending much time assessing individual claims on an accelerated timetable at the beginning of the case might be inefficient in this context, given the high likelihood that the court would throw out the litigation in its entirety based either on the preemption defense or a lack of reliable evidence demonstrating causation. Nonetheless, as critics of the current system would note, flexibility has often led to significant problems in MDL cases, with MDL courts exercising their discretion in ways that are counterproductive.

As a result, many knowledgeable participants in MDL proceedings—particularly those in the defense bar and the corporate community—maintain that there is an urgent need for reform. In their view, while there may be examples of MDLs that have been successful, the problem is that there are many MDLs that have failed. They maintain that the current system imposes undue pressure on defendants to settle, regardless of the merits of the underlying claims. Moreover, they assert that it is not uncommon for large percentages of the claims to be meritless. As a result, they suggest that defendants increasingly will choose essentially to opt out of MDLs by refusing to settle and seeking remand of the underlying claims. Accordingly, there is a wide divergence of views regarding whether reform of the rules and statutes governing MDL proceedings is needed.

In the meantime, there are many efforts underway to improve MDL proceedings. There are a variety of conferences and other gatherings of regular participants in MDL proceedings that have been dedicated to education and discussion regarding the procedures employed in those proceedings. Organizations such as Duke Law School's Bolch Judicial Institute have gone further, attempting to draft guidelines that recommend best practices for MDL proceedings.

As MDL procedures continue to evolve, there is an increasing recognition that there are problems in the current system that should be addressed to increase the efficiency and justice of the proceedings. The question that remains is how to best accomplish these goals.

11
Alternatives to Multidistrict Litigation

The recent debate over MDL procedure and the perceived problems with the MDL system have spurred increasing interest in alternatives to MDL proceedings. However, as the increase in the number and scope of MDL proceedings would suggest, there are no perfect alternatives, and it is unlikely that other procedural mechanisms for addressing mass tort claims will supplant multidistrict litigation in the future. Nonetheless, there has been some movement in this direction, and it bears discussion, as multidistrict litigation continues to undergo change.

Litigation of Individual Claims

The most obvious alternative to multidistrict litigation is individual litigation of claims. This is a theoretical alternative to an MDL proceeding, given that the MDL statute provides that MDL consolidation is for "pretrial" proceedings and expressly provides for remand of cases back to the courts from which they were transferred at the end of the proceedings. Accordingly, while a party may be successful in having the JPML establish an MDL proceeding, there is no guarantee the proceeding will result in resolution of the entire litigation, either through settlement or through litigation before the MDL court. Rather, pre-trial proceedings may be conducted and, at the end of the process, the cases may be remanded to the transferor courts for resolution. This could occur, for example, where the parties fail to enter into a global settlement. Indeed, the MDL statute provides that cases consolidated in an MDL proceeding "shall be remanded . . . at or before the conclusion of such pretrial proceedings."[284] As one court has observed, "[t]his mandatory language creates a powerful presumption in favor of remand, one that cannot easily be overcome. The result is a statutory right to remand following an MDL proceeding, analogous to the statutory right to removal under 28 U.S.C. § 1441."[285]

To date, this has not been the predominant means by which cases transferred to an MDL proceeding are resolved. Duke Law School's Bolch Judicial Institute has calculated, based on publicly available data, that "96% of the individual actions consolidated in MDLs are terminated by the MDL transferee judges" either through settlement or litigation.[286] Thus, the vast majority of cases that have been transferred into an MDL are not remanded back to the courts where they were filed. In sum, "[i]t remains true that the great majority of cases are resolved in the transferee forum, and that most are resolved by some sort of settlement."[287]

Despite this record, there appears to be an increasing willingness to consider remand: "Although global resolution remains a goal of most MDLs, for today's MDL judge, strategic planning and efficient management of the process at every stage is the touchstone of success. Likewise, resolution of the case increasingly includes the possibility of not only settlement, but also dismissal or remand."[288] Accordingly, "courts are now mindful of and prepared for the possibility of remand if cases are not otherwise resolved. There is no longer a stigma attached to remanding cases when they are ready for trial if the parties are not ready to settle. Indeed, this was the original legislative directive in creating the MDL device."[289]

Advocates of remand argue that it has many advantages over global settlement of an MDL proceeding. These advantages are tied, in part, to the fact that remand inherently disaggregates the litigation by sending individual cases back to federal courts across the country. As one commentator has explained, "[p]rocedurally, disaggregating can help correct error by bypassing private, global settlements that are inherently non-appealable, building secondary judicial review into the process and incorporating pluralistic fact-finding by jurors on plaintiff-specific and state-specific issues."[290]

Remand presents the opportunity for many different courts to involve themselves with determining the merits of the cases. While the MDL court's rulings may be law of the case, the possibility exists for these courts to revisit those rulings, and if these cases proceed to completion, there is the possibility of review by multiple appellate courts of the individual cases. Likewise, there is the potential for trials that involve multiple juries drawn from different locations across the country, assessing the facts of the cases and determining whether there is liability and, if so, the appropriate amount of any damages. While such proceedings may be more costly and time consuming, they certainly increase and diversify the attention paid to each individual case.

In fact, remand is required by the MDL statute when other avenues have failed. The MDL court is not supposed to retain jurisdiction over the cases indefinitely. As the Federal Judicial Center has observed, "[r]emand is required when centralized proceedings have concluded, but one or more transferred cases remain unresolved."[291] Accordingly, the Federal Judicial Center recommends that MDL courts view remand as a viable and, in some instances, required option: "When discovery has been completed, pretrial motions have been ruled upon, and reasonable attempts to try or settle the actions have not borne fruit, your final responsibility is to recommend that the Panel remand those unresolved cases to their transferor districts. When coordinated or consolidated pretrial proceedings no longer serve a valid purpose, do not hesitate in making this recommendation."[292]

Indeed, some commentators have argued that holding cases too tightly in an MDL proceeding can even raise constitutional concerns: "Limiting plaintiffs' freedom to select their forum, sending them to a place that would ordinarily lack personal jurisdiction over them, and retaining their cases indefinitely such that returning home for trial is a near impossibility raises constitutional questions."[293] While such constitutional concerns receive little attention in the real world of mass litigation, there certainly are, at a minimum, prudential and practical concerns raised by MDL consolidation that warrant consideration. It may be that in some cases remand is the best solution and, indeed, those involved in the process and MDL courts themselves appear to increasingly recognize that this is the case.

Moreover, the potential downsides of remand can be mitigated to some extent by the MDL court, which can take a number of steps to make the remand function proceed more smoothly. First, if the court has addressed the significant pre-trial issues, including dispositive motions, the court will have achieved much of the efficiency contemplated under the MDL statute. The court may eliminate categories of claims or issues from the litigation by resolving dispositive pre-trial motions, significantly narrowing the scope of the litigation. Even where the MDL court denies dispositive motions, the court has at least done the work that potentially hundreds of other judges would have had to perform in one stroke. These judges can then pick up where the MDL court left off.

In addition, in remanding the cases, the MDL court can provide guidance in a final remand memorandum, summarizing the history of the MDL proceedings and generally imparting the knowledge the MDL court has gained to the transferor courts that will preside over the litigation: "Remand packets, which are generally entered with the suggestion of remand in the form of a case-management or pretrial order, have been recognized as particularly valuable to transferor courts because they encapsulate and describe the relevant proceedings and suggest a path for the transferor courts going forward."[294]

More fundamentally, in many disputes that result in the creation of an MDL, there is already individual litigation outside of the MDL system. Whereas in the past there was a fair amount of discipline among the plaintiff's bar to join in an MDL once it was established, today there appears to be a greater degree of individual litigation outside the MDL process. There are a number of examples where individual cases have been tried outside MDLs, and there may be an emerging trend toward such increased decentralization.[295]

In the future, it may be defendants who more readily seek individual resolution over an MDL proceeding. There are, however, certain downsides to this approach. First, defendants would lose the efficiency of the MDL proceeding. They would have to defend multiple individual cases in front of different judges across the country who may not coordinate their proceedings with one another. Such litigation could quickly devolve into chaos as each plaintiff seeks an early trial date for that plaintiff's claims, resulting in the possibility of multiple, early, and simultaneous trials.

Moreover, if individual litigation dominates, plaintiffs can always engage in forum shopping in an attempt to file their cases in the best possible judicial forum. Plaintiffs will select plaintiff-friendly jurisdictions where they can obtain large judgments, thereby making individual litigation an undesirable outcome. Nonetheless, at the same time there is a cost to the plaintiffs of pursuing individual litigation. Just as it can be costly for defendants, it can also be costly for plaintiff counsel, who must advance the costs of the litigation. Where defendants prevail at trial, continued litigation of individual cases may become less desirable. Moreover, not all plaintiff firms are created equal, and many may lack the resources necessary to pursue cases on an individual basis, whereas they would be more than happy to free-ride off other plaintiff firms in a consolidated MDL proceeding.

Class Action

Another potential alternative to multidistrict litigation is the class action device. Under Rule 23, a plaintiff may file a complaint in which the plaintiff seeks to represent a class of individuals who have similar characteristics. The class action procedure therefore provides a mechanism for pursuing aggregate litigation in a single case. There are fairly stringent requirements for pursuing a class action, however, which must be certified by the court presiding over the litigation. There must be a sufficient number of potential plaintiffs who are members of the class, the claims of the class members must share common issues, the claim of the named plaintiff bringing the lawsuit must be typical of the other members of the class, and the named plaintiff must be an adequate representative of the interests of the class.[296] In addition, the common issues among class members must generally predominate over other issues in the litigation to invoke the class action procedure.[297]

Supreme Court precedent interpreting the Federal Rules of Civil Procedure significantly limits the ability of plaintiffs to utilize the class action device in personal injury cases. In *Amchem Products, Inc. v. Windsor*[298] and *Ortiz v. Fibreboard Corp.*,[299] the Supreme Court observed that class actions inherently involve facts that are largely individualized. Individual plaintiffs have different levels of information regarding the risks of the products they used; they may have different injuries; and they may have different damages. Individual plaintiffs may be exposed to a variety of different potential causes of their injury. In addition, because of these individualized differences, there may be conflicts of interest among the members of the class.

Accordingly, the class action device is typically inappropriate for resolution of the sort of litigation that is the subject of many MDL proceedings: "in most mass tort cases today, granting of class certification is unlikely."[300] As the Federal Judicial Center has recognized, "[m]ass tort personal injury cases are rarely appropriate for class certification for trial, particularly on a nationwide or multistate basis, because individual issues of causation and individual damages often predominate and state law often varies."[301] Indeed, the evolution of the law regarding class certification toward a more restrictive standard is arguably one of the factors leading to the rise in multidistrict litigation: "As use of the class action device to aggregate claims has become more difficult, MDL consolidation has increased in importance as a means of achieving final, global resolution of mass national disputes."[302]

Despite these barriers to class certification, increasingly plaintiffs are seeking to bring economic loss claims alleging that, because products were defective, they are less valuable than the plaintiffs believed and accordingly plaintiffs have suffered economic injury. Such claims may be brought as an appendage to personal injury litigation alleging that the product caused injury or disease. However, they may also be brought in circumstances where there is no personal injury, but rather only a defective product that plaintiffs allege is less valuable. While the prevalence of such litigation appears to be increasing, attempts to certify such cases as class actions face many of the same hurdles presented with respect to purported personal injury class actions.

Moreover, despite the recent trend in such litigation, absent some sort of reform of the rules, the class action device likely will never be a viable mechanism for the largest category of multidistrict litigation—personal injury claims. A long line of judicial precedent bars attempts to certify such claims as a class action. Nonetheless, parties have attempted to nudge the system in this direction. For example, the court in the *National Prescription Opiate* MDL contemplated a "negotiation" class to reach a consensual settlement of that litigation. One theory behind such efforts is the belief that the requirements for certification may be relaxed in the context of a potential settlement. And, indeed, even some conservative academics have advocated a renewed look at the class action mechanism as a potentially beneficial procedural device for the resolution of certain sorts of litigation.[303] Nonetheless, under current law, absent changes to the rules, certification of a litigation class is not a viable mechanism for resolving large mass tort proceedings.

Bankruptcy

A final mechanism for potentially resolving mass tort claims is more extreme, but is increasingly being used as the civil litigation system fails to efficiently resolve such claims.[304] Companies are increasingly seeking to address large mass tort claims in the bankruptcy system, where streamlined procedures allow these claims to be addressed efficiently and defendants may obtain an order discharging any further liability for the claims.[305] This procedural option provides some measure of certainty and finality to mass tort liability. It also allows a company to reorganize while under the protection of the bankruptcy laws, which stay all pending claims, instead of facing a Wild West scenario of potentially thousands of claims filed all over the country. This automatic stay of the litigation by itself is a significant benefit to a company entering bankruptcy. The stay is designed to preserve the debtor's assets by "protect[ing] debtors from creditors and creditors from each other."[306] Not only does it prevent continuing chaos, but it saves a company substantial litigation costs that might otherwise significantly impair the value of the corporation and, ultimately, may detract from any payment to tort claimants.

Bankruptcy provides some of the same advantages as the MDL procedure. In bankruptcy, litigation is centralized before a single bankruptcy judge and overseen by a district judge presiding over the litigation.[307] All claims are therefore resolved in a single forum, obtaining the same efficiencies that would be obtained by centralization before an MDL court. However, the efficiencies may be even greater in a bankruptcy proceeding. For example, the bankruptcy court can reach out and stay state court litigation that would otherwise continue in parallel with a federal MDL proceeding. It therefore provides a mechanism for solving the problem of coordination between federal and state courts.

In addition, bankruptcy courts enjoy broad jurisdiction, which they may exercise over all claims related to the bankruptcy proceeding.[308] Accordingly, bankruptcy courts may exercise jurisdiction not only over claims brought against the debtor itself, but also over claims brought against third parties where the claims are related to the bankruptcy proceedings. This broad jurisdictional authority allows bankruptcy courts to stay litigation against third parties, as well as transfer claims against third parties to the bankruptcy court for resolution. As a result, as commentators have observed, "it is plain that the filing of bankruptcy, together with the broad reach of the 'related to' jurisdictional provision and the transfer power, provides a very potent tool for aggregation and global resolution in connection with Chapter 11 reorganization."[309]

Moreover, bankruptcy courts frequently employ streamlined procedures for the resolution of claims that may not be available outside the bankruptcy system. For example, bankruptcy courts may estimate mass tort claims rather than litigating them. The estimate is used to fund a post-confirmation trust that will pay any asserted claims, while the bankruptcy court issues an order freeing the debtor from any remaining liability. Such procedures can be used to resolve large numbers of claims efficiently in a comparatively short amount of time. Bankruptcy therefore has certain potential advantages over multidistrict litigation.

Bankruptcy also, however, has certain obvious potential disadvantages. There are costs to putting a company into Chapter 11 bankruptcy proceedings. The business may be disrupted, relationships with other corporate creditors may be damaged, and there can be reputational damage to a corporation entering bankruptcy. Accordingly, for most companies, absent the most overwhelming mass tort litigation, bankruptcy will not be a preferable option. Nonetheless, there are certain circumstances in which this procedural mechanism has been used to successfully resolve mass tort liability, and recent mass tort bankruptcies have received significant attention.

There is, for example, a long history of resolving asbestos personal injury claims in the bankruptcy system. Since the bankruptcy of Johns-Manville in the 1980s, numerous companies have sought to resolve their asbestos liability through the bankruptcy system. Asbestos cases involved a notorious mass tort that continued to expand to new defendants over the decades. As the original manufacturers of asbestos went into bankruptcy, plaintiffs searched for more tangential defendants that may have acquired companies with a relationship to asbestos or may have incorporated asbestos into some of their products. As a result, there have been waves of corporate bankruptcies as each new company falls like a domino in a row into the bankruptcy system.

This phenomenon only accelerated when Congress passed legislation to facilitate the use of the bankruptcy system to resolve asbestos liability. As noted, claims in mass tort bankruptcies are typically channeled to a trust established to pay them after the bankruptcy is completed. The bankrupt company then emerges with a release from any liability, which is channeled to the trust.

Because there was some uncertainty regarding the solidity of such channeling injunctions, Congress sought to make clear by statute that, if certain conditions were met, asbestos liabilities could be channeled to such a trust irrevocably without recourse to the debtor. Congress did so in the Bankruptcy Reform Act of 1994, which prescribed certain requirements for obtaining a release of liability for asbestos tort claims under Chapter 11.[310] As a result of this legislation, there was a clear path for companies seeking to resolve their asbestos liability in the bankruptcy system, and they took advantage of it.

In the meantime, the use of the MDL procedure to resolve asbestos liability fell by the wayside. As noted, when Judge Robreno was appointed to oversee the federal asbestos MDL, there were literally thousands of claims clogging the system, with more emerging every day. Judge Robreno began the hard work of evaluating each claim on an individual basis, eventually terminating the MDL after resolving the individual cases. Accordingly, the use of an MDL to address asbestos liability ended, as the use of the bankruptcy system emerged as the dominant means by which such claims were resolved. Now, there is essentially a system under which companies seek to settle their claims on an ongoing basis, sometimes pursuing trials, with one eye on bankruptcy as the ultimate means of resolving their asbestos liability.

Asbestos litigation is not the only mass tort that has spawned bankruptcy proceedings. There have been many instances in which companies have resorted to the bankruptcy system to resolve company-threatening liability, including some recent high-profile bankruptcy filings. One of the most famous examples was the Dow Corning bankruptcy, which was spawned by allegations that the company's silicone breast implants caused a variety of autoimmune diseases.[311] While the scientific case was eventually proven meritless, the company faced thousands of personal injury tort cases that were flooding the court system. Despite the existence of a federal MDL to address breast implant liability, the company determined that the bankruptcy system was the optimal solution. Accordingly, it initiated the bankruptcy process, passing through Chapter 11 and establishing a trust to fund the payment of breast implant claims based on predetermined criteria. The bankruptcy gave the company room while the science emerged. As studies began to show no relationship between silicone breast implants and autoimmune diseases, the emerging science impacted the value of the claims in the bankruptcy proceedings, ultimately reducing the amounts paid to tort claimants. At the same time, the company saved significant litigation costs by staying litigation that threatened to proceed on multiple fronts across the country. While the company's plan of reorganization provided a track for claimants who wished to opt out of the settlement process provided in Dow Corning's plan of reorganization and litigate their claims in court, given the evolving science, hardly any claimants chose to do so.

Another example is the A.H. Robins bankruptcy, which was precipitated by lawsuits alleging that the company's Dalkon Shield IUD was defective. This was one of the first large mass tort bankruptcies and was resolved successfully. Numerous claims against the company, many of which also named doctors and hospitals as defendants, were resolved through Chapter 11 proceedings. This is one of the first examples of a mass tort bankruptcy in which the court utilized its broad jurisdiction over all claims related to the bankruptcy to resolve claims not only against the debtor but also against third-party co-defendants. The court held that, "pursuant to Section 1334(b), all actions based upon personal injury tort or wrongful death claims arising from the use of the Dalkon Shield were proceedings 'related to' [A.H. Robins's] Chapter 11 case."[312] Having centralized the litigation in one forum, the court then effectively resolved it, establishing a trust to pay all claims alleging injury from the Dalkon Shield device.

The A.H. Robins bankruptcy illustrates how, to some extent, mass tort bankruptcy proceedings parallel MDL proceedings. As in an MDL proceeding, claimants typically provide initial information regarding their claims in a proof of claim they file with the court. In the A.H. Robins bankruptcy, the court required, among other things, information regarding "the claimant's use of the Dalkon Shield, such as . . . the type of injury alleged and the names of physicians or clinics visited by the claimant."[313] This information could then be used to evaluate the claims and determine whether they were eligible for compensation.

Much like Dow Corning, the company set up a trust to pay tort claimants who alleged injury from the Dalkon Shield device after the company emerged from bankruptcy. A channeling injunction directed those claims to the trust and away from the company. Claimants could elect to litigate or arbitrate their claims, rather than submitting them to the trust. However, of the more than 350,000 claims filed, only 6,600 chose to opt out of the settlement and pursue this litigation alternative.[314] The trust paid all of the asserted claims with money left to spare.[315] Accordingly, the company utilized the Bankruptcy Code to efficiently resolve its tort liability, as well as the tort liability of others implicated in the lawsuits that were flooding the court system.

Other recent high-profile bankruptcy filings have been occasioned by large-scale mass tort litigation involving talc and opioids. For example, Imerys Talc America sought Chapter 11 protection after it was faced with lawsuits alleging that its talc was contaminated with asbestos.[316] Similarly, opioid manufacturer Insys Therapeutics sought bankruptcy protection after it was faced with a wave of litigation alleging that its opioid products resulted in addiction and had entered into a settlement agreement with the federal government for allegedly bribing physicians to prescribe its medication.[317] Purdue Pharma, another manufacturer of opioids, followed Insys Therapeutics into the bankruptcy system, filing its own Chapter 11 proceedings.[318]

These examples illustrate that, while bankruptcy may not be a viable option for most defendants caught up in mass tort litigation, it increasingly is a desirable option for many companies seeking to resolve such liability. Bankruptcy frequently serves as a superior mechanism for centralization of mass tort litigation. It provides the debtor company with breathing room by staying the litigation. Moreover, it frequently provides an efficient mechanism for resolution of large-scale liability that can be comparable, or superior, to resolution outside the bankruptcy system. Accordingly, absent significant reform, in the future we may see increasing use of bankruptcy as an alternative to multidistrict litigation.

Conclusion

Large-scale litigation, such as that involving mass torts, presents potential challenges for any system of dispute resolution. The sheer number of claims and the individual differences among them make it difficult to come to a just resolution. Such litigation involves thousands of individual parties with their own unique interests in the litigation and the potential for significant disagreements regarding the appropriate path toward resolution.

These challenges are reflected in the current debate over multidistrict litigation in the federal system. The problems critics have identified in the MDL process are emblematic of problems more generally with the resolution of such mass litigations. State and federal courts have grappled with some of these same issues for decades as they have addressed mass torts involving asbestos, breast implants, pharmaceuticals, medical devices, and many other products and exposures. The fact that multidistrict litigation does not present a perfect vehicle for resolving such large-sale litigation is not surprising. Other means of resolving such disputes have been tried, and no perfect solution has been found.

This does not mean the system cannot be improved, however. As the current debate over multidistrict litigation demonstrates, many participants in the current system have given significant thought to the ways in which it can be made more just and efficient. Lawyers representing plaintiffs and defendants, the business community, judges, and academics have all provided suggestions regarding ways in which the system can be improved. This debate is welcome. For many years, there was a lack of recognition of the problems surrounding multidistrict litigation and, thus, a lack of attention to resolving them. Now, at least, there is a general recognition that there are significant problems in modern MDL practice.

The question arises as to how best to solve these problems. Is it better to continue to allow judges to craft their own solutions exercising their discretion, or would it be better to make formal amendments to the rules or statutes that would take discretion away from MDL judges and impose a mandatory framework that governs certain aspects of MDL proceedings? Right now, there is a significant debate regarding whether to implement revisions to the statutes and rules that frame multidistrict litigation. Statutory changes can be difficult to achieve in our polarized political system, particularly given that this is a topic that involves a variety of different interests with significant financial stakes. Likewise, there may be resistance from some members of the judiciary who may want to preserve their freedom and flexibility to address circumstances as they arise in large MDL proceedings. On the other hand, there appears to be a consensus among many participants in MDL proceedings that there are significant problems in the current MDL system and that reforms to MDL procedures may be warranted. It remains to be seen whether, and to what extent, formal changes to the rules and statutes governing MDL proceedings will be implemented.

In addition, however, there have been renewed efforts to implement informal changes to the MDL system. Guidelines and best practices have proliferated as the participants in MDL cases have come together to attempt to collect their knowledge of what has worked and what has not, and then transfer that knowledge to courts who are assigned MDL cases. Judges have approached MDL cases with a spirit of innovation, eager to try new procedures that may more efficiently and expeditiously resolve multidistrict litigation. Accordingly, change may come from these more informal proposals adopted from the ground up on a case-by-case basis by individual judges seeking to improve the system.

The question arises as to which model is going to dominate the MDL landscape moving forward. Are we going to see more courts shift back toward a traditional adversarial model that fully implements the Federal Rules of Civil Procedure to scrutinize the merits of the asserted claims and weed out claims that lack merit using the normal tools available in civil litigation in the federal courts? Or are we going to see more courts moving in the opposite direction, attempting to encourage or even force global settlements, regardless of the merits of the underlying claims? We have seen recent examples of both models, and to some extent there may be some degree of polarization within the federal system, with some courts going in one direction while others go in the opposite direction. Absent formal amendments to the legal rules governing MDL proceedings, there will be room for both models in the federal system. Moreover, it may be that courts view one model or the other as being more appropriate depending on the nature of the particular MDL before them.

Nonetheless, as this book has attempted to illustrate, the traditional model is arguably the better one. Many courts have utilized the normal rules of civil procedure to efficiently and effectively resolve large-scale MDL proceedings. While some reforms of the current system may be warranted and may improve the efficiency of the MDL process significantly, the existing rules of civil procedure certainly provide powerful tools for courts seeking to resolve MDL proceedings, and there are many examples of MDL courts effectively utilizing these rules to bring MDL cases to an efficient and just conclusion.

To the extent MDL cases have run into trouble, in many cases it can be traced to a failure to apply the normal rules of procedure. In instances where courts have moved away from the traditional adversarial model and employed a more active judicial role, perhaps in the hope that litigation can be resolved through settlement facilitated by a more active court, cases have tended to linger. Moreover, even where such settlements are reached, in many cases there have been objections that there was an element of coercion. Accordingly, there are good reasons not to deviate from the traditional model that governs litigation in our adversarial system.

However, this does not mean that the procedures courts utilize within this framework cannot be improved or that there is no room for innovation. As we have seen, many courts have developed innovative procedures for resolving cases through their normal case-management powers. Courts have developed procedures such as fact sheets, administrative and show cause orders, use of magistrates, *Lone Pine* orders, encouraging voluntary settlement, and threat of sanctions to improve the efficiency of large-scale multidistrict litigation. These innovations represent the normal exercise of judicial authority to improve case management, and such measures will likely continue to further improve MDL proceedings.

One potential innovation that has received somewhat less attention is to improve the transparency of the MDL process. There is currently a lack of complete transparency, especially with respect to settlement, in large MDL proceedings. One way in which transparency has been increased is by publicizing the procedures MDL courts have used to resolve large MDL cases, which, in turn, has led to the dissemination of guidelines and best practices. To the extent judges and participants in an MDL are aware of what has been done in prior MDLs, it can only improve the process.

However, there is certainly room for further transparency. One potential measure would be for courts to collect and publicize data regarding MDL settlements. As noted, there is anecdotal evidence that many plaintiffs in MDL cases never obtain any compensation in large settlements. Rather, many claimants do not satisfy the criteria for receiving settlement compensation—apparently in the neighborhood of 30 to 40 percent. This is important information to know, for a variety of reasons. If courts were aware that a large percentage of claims filed in large MDLs never receive compensation because they cannot meet even minimal settlement criteria, they might take more seriously their obligation to litigate the merits of the claims before them. Moreover, plaintiffs would be made aware that filing a claim was no guarantee of receiving compensation, even if there were a settlement, which might reduce the filing of unsupported claims. Finally, more attention could be paid to how settlement compensation is allocated. From a plaintiff advocate perspective, these numbers may suggest that there is some degree of unfairness or inequity in the allocation of settlement payments in large MDL proceedings. At a minimum, increased transparency can only improve the process.

Whatever the answer to these questions in the coming years, it is certain that multidistrict litigation will continue to play an important role in resolving large-scale litigation in the federal court system. Moreover, the procedures employed by MDL courts will likely have some impact on similar proceedings, such as consolidated proceedings in state courts that increasingly mirror MDL proceedings. Accordingly, the attention given to MDL procedure is more than warranted. One can only hope that it will lead to increasingly efficient and just outcomes in resolving multidistrict litigation.

Endnotes

1. Duke Law Center for Judicial Studies, *MDL Standards and Best Practices* xi (Sept. 11, 2014) (MDLs represent 45.6% of pending civil cases as of June 2014); Bolch Judicial Institute, Duke Law School, *Guidelines and Best Practices for Large and Mass-Tort MDLs* vi–vii (2d ed. 2018) [hereinafter Bolch Judicial Institute, *Guidelines and Best Practices*].
2. Pub. L. 90–296 (1968), 28 U.S.C. § 1407.
3. *Gelboim v. Bank of Am. Corp.*, 574 U.S. 405, 410 (2015).
4. Andrew D. Bradt & D. Theodore Rave, *The Information-Forcing Role of the Judge in Multidistrict Litigation*, 105 Cal. L. Rev. 1259, 1261 (2017).
5. Bolch Judicial Institute, *Guidelines and Best Practices* at vi–vii.
6. 28 U.S.C. § 1407.
7. *See* Lawyers for Civil Justice, *Request for Rulemaking to the Advisory Committee on Civil Rules* 12 (Aug. 10, 2017).
8. 28 U.S.C. § 1407.
9. *See, e.g., In re Plavix Mktg., Sales Practices and Prods. Liab. Litig.*, 923 F. Supp. 2d 1376 (J.P.M.L. 2013).
10. *In re Scotch Whiskey*, 299 F. Supp. 543, 544 (J.P.M.L. 2011).
11. *In re Spray Polyurethane Foam Insulation Prods. Liab. Litig.*, 949 F. Supp. 2d 1364, 1364 (J.P.M.L. 2013).
12. *See* 28 U.S.C. § 1407.
13. *See, e.g., In re Petition of Boehringer Ingelheim Pharms., Inc. and Boehringer Ingelheim Int'l GMBH, in Pradaxa (Dabigatran Etexilate) Prods. Liab. Litig.*, 745 F.3d 216 (7th Cir. 2014).
14. *See, e.g., In re Toyota Motor Corp. Unintended Acceleration Mktg. Sales Practices & Prods. Liab. Litig.*, 704 F. Supp. 2d 1379, 1382 (J.P.M.L. 2010).
15. *See* David F. Herr & Nicole Narotzky, *The Judicial Panel's Role in Managing Mass Litigation*, ALI-ABA Course of Study (May 29–31, 2008).
16. Washington Legal Foundation, *Multidistrict Litigation: Reducing Incentives for Abuse* 1 (Autumn 2017).
17. *See* Douglas G. Smith, *The Myth of Settlement in MDL Proceedings*, 107 Ky. L.J. 467, 471–72 (2019).

18. Washington Legal Foundation, *Multidistrict Litigation: Reducing Incentives for Abuse* 2 (Autumn 2017).
19. *In re Mentor Corp. Obtape Transobturator Sling Prods. Liab. Litig.*, No. 4: 08-MD-2004, 2016 WL 4705827, at *2 (M.D. Ga. Sept. 7, 2016).
20. *Id.* at *1.
21. *See* Andrew D. Bradt & D. Theodore Rave, *The Information-Forcing Role of the Judge in Multidistrict Litigation*, 105 CAL. L. REV. 1259 (2017).
22. United States Chamber Institute for Legal Reform, *MDL Proceedings: Eliminating the Chaff* 1 (2015).
23. Elizabeth Chamblee Burch, *Mass Tort Deals: Backroom Bargaining in Multidistrict Litigation* (2019) [hereinafter Burch, *Mass Tort Deals*].
24. Martin H. Redish & Julie M. Karaba, *One Size Doesn't Fit All: Multidistrict Litigation, Due Process, and the Dangers of Procedural Collectivism*, 95 B.U. L. REV. 109, 151 (2015).
25. Eduardo C. Robreno, *The Federal Asbestos Product Liability Multidistrict Litigation (MDL-875): Black Hole or New Paradigm?* 23 WIDENER L.J. 97, 187 (2013).
26. *In re Mentor Corp. Obtape Transobturator Sling*, 2016 WL 4705827, at *1–2.
27. *In re Seroquel Prods. Liab. Litig.*, 447 F. Supp. 2d 1376, 1379 (J.P.M.L. 2006).
28. *In re Cook Med., Inc. IVC Filters Mktg., Sales Practices and Prods. Liab. Litig.*, 53 F. Supp. 3d 1379, 1381 (J.P.M.L. 2014).
29. Eldon E. Fallon et al., *Bellwether Trials in Multidistrict Litigation*, 82 TULANE L. REV. 2323, 2333–34 (2008).
30. Elizabeth Chamblee Burch, *Monopolies in Multidistrict Litigation*, 70 VAND. L. REV. 67, 74–75 (2017).
31. Burch, *Mass Tort Deals* at 54–55.
32. *See* Fed. R. Evid. 702.
33. *See* Eldon E. Fallon et al., *Bellwether Trials in Multidistrict Litigation*, 82 TUL. L. REV. 2323, 2333 (2008).
34. Washington Legal Foundation, *Multidistrict Litigation: Reducing Incentives for Abuse* 6 (Autumn 2017).
35. Lawyers for Civil Justice, *Request for Rulemaking* 4 (Aug. 10, 2017).
36. Barbara J. Rothstein & Catherine R. Borden, Federal Judicial Center, *Managing Multidistrict Litigation in Products Liability Cases: A Pocket Guide for Transferee Judges* 44 (2011) [hereinafter Federal Judicial Center, *Pocket Guide*].
37. *See, e.g.*, Thomas Sekula, note, *Selective Settlement and the Integrity of the Bellwether Process*, 97 TEX. L. REV. 859 (2019).
38. Burch, *Mass Tort Deals* at 74.
39. *In re Cook Med., Inc., IVC Filters*, 53 F. Supp. 3d at 1381.
40. *See* Amanda Bronstad, *Rookie Judges Start to Wrangle MDL Dockets*, Law.com (Apr. 17, 2017).
41. United States Judicial Panel on Multidistrict Litigation, Federal Judicial Center, *Ten Steps to Better Case Management: A Guide for Multidistrict Litigation Transferee Judges* v (2d ed. 2014) [hereinafter Federal Judicial Center, *Ten Steps*].
42. Bolch Judicial Institute, *Guidelines and Best Practices* at vi.
43. Federal Judicial Center, *Ten Steps* at 3.
44. Bolch Judicial Institute, *Guidelines and Best Practices* at 2.

45. Federal Judicial Center, *Pocket Guide* at 8.
46. *Id.* at 6.
47. Federal Judicial Center, *Ten Steps* at 1.
48. Federal Judicial Center, *Pocket Guide* at 7.
49. Fed. R. Civ. P. 16.
50. Federal Judicial Center, *Manual for Complex Litigation*, Fourth § 22.634 (2004).
51. *Id.*
52. Fed. R. Civ. P. 16(c)(2)(A).
53. *See* J.P.M.L. Rule 7.1.
54. Federal Judicial Center, *Pocket Guide* at 2.
55. Bolch Judicial Institute, *Guidelines and Best Practices* at 3.
56. Federal Judicial Center, *Pocket Guide* at 4.
57. *Id.* at 38.
58. Federal Judicial Center, *Reference Manual on Scientific Evidence* 7–8 (3d ed. 2011).
59. Federal Judicial Center, *Pocket Guide* at 39.
60. Bolch Judicial Institute, *Guidelines and Best Practices* at 4.
61. *Id.*
62. *Id.*
63. Burch, *Mass Tort Deals* at 144–45.
64. Federal Judicial Center, *Pocket Guide* at 10.
65. *Id.* at 14 n.18, 15.
66. Martin H. Redish & Julie M. Karaba, *One Size Doesn't Fit All: Multidistrict Litigation, Due Process, and the Dangers of Procedural Collectivism*, 95 B.U. L. Rev. 109, 124 (2015).
67. Federal Judicial Center, *Pocket Guide* at 2.
68. Bolch Judicial Institute, *Guidelines and Best Practices* at 38.
69. Burch, *Mass Tort Deals* at 19.
70. Eldon E. Fallon, *Common Benefit Fees in Multidistrict Litigation*, 74 La. L. Rev. 371, 386 (2014).
71. Bolch Judicial Institute, *Guidelines and Best Practices* at 61.
72. *Id.* at 9.
73. *Id.*
74. *Id.*
75. *Id.* at 10.
76. *Id.*
77. *See* Fed. R. Evid. 11.
78. *See* Bolch Judicial Institute, *Guidelines and Best Practices* at 11.
79. *Id.*
80. *See In re Nat'l Prescription Opiate Litig.*, 956 F.3d 838 (6th Cir. 2020).
81. Bolch Judicial Institute, *Guidelines and Best Practices* at 12.
82. *Id.* at 14.
83. *Id.* at 12.
84. Case Management Order No. 12 (Product Identification Order), *In re: Taxotere (Docetaxel) Prods. Liab. Litig.*, No. 2:16-md-02740, at 1 (E.D. La. Jan. 12, 2018), E.C.F. No. 1506.
85. *Id.* at 5.

86. *See id.* at 6.
87. *Merck Sharp & Dohme Corp. v. Albrecht*, 139 S. Ct. 1668, 1680 (2019).
88. *See* Initial Case Management Scheduling Order re General Causation at 1-2, *In re: Incretin Mimetics Prods. Liab. Litig.*, No. 13-MD-2452 (S.D. Cal. Feb. 18, 2014), ECF No. 325.
89. Federal Judicial Center, *Pocket Guide* at 17.
90. *See Wal-Mart Stores, Inc. v. Dukes*, 564 U.S. 338 (2011).
91. *See In re Meridia Prods. Liab. Litig.*, 328 F. Supp. 2d 791 (N.D. Ohio 2004).
92. Bolch Judicial Institute, *Guidelines and Best Practices* at 6–7 (quoting S. Todd Brown, *Plaintiff Control & Domination in Multidistrict Mass Torts*, 61 CLEV. ST. L. REV. 391, 399 (2013)).
93. *See generally* Mark Herrmann et al., Statewide Coordinated Proceedings: State Court Analogues to the Federal MDL Process (2d ed. 2004).
94. *See, e.g.*, Burch, *Mass Tort Deals.*
95. Martin H. Redish & Julie M. Karaba, *One Size Doesn't Fit All: Multidistrict Litigation, Due Process, and the Dangers of Procedural Collectivism*, 95 B.U. L. REV. 109, 110 (2015).
96. U.S. Chamber Institute for Legal Reform, *Trials and Tribulations: Contending with Bellwether and Multi-Plaintiff Trials in MDL Plaintiffs* 1 (Oct. 2019).
97. Bolch Judicial Institute, *Guidelines and Best Practices* at 17.
98. Federal Judicial Center, *Ten Steps* at 4.
99. *Gelboim*, 135 S. Ct. at 904–05 (modifications to quoted text and emphasis in the original).
100. Eduardo C. Robreno, *The Federal Asbestos Product Liability Multidistrict Litigation (MDL-875): Black Hole or New Paradigm?* 23 WIDENER L.J. 97, 186 (2013).
101. Federal Judicial Center, *Pocket Guide* at 3.
102. Duke Law School Center for Judicial Studies, *MDL Standards and Best Practices* 6 (Sept. 11, 2014).
103. *See* Douglas G. Smith, *Resolution of Common Questions in MDL Proceedings*, 66 U. KAN. L. REV. 219 (2017).
104. Burch, *Mass Tort Deals.*
105. *In re Lipitor (Atorvastatin Calcium) Mktg., Sales Practices and Prods. Liab. Litig.*, 227 F. Supp. 3d 452, 463, 491 (D.S.C. 2017).
106. *Id.* at 457.
107. *In re Mirena IUD Prods. Liab. Litig.*, 169 F. Supp. 3d 396, 430 (S.D.N.Y. 2016).
108. *Id.* at 426–27.
109. *In re Phenylpropanolamine (PPA) Prods. Liab. Litig.*, 289 F. Supp. 2d 1230 (W.D. Wash. 2003).
110. Barbara J. Rothstein et al., *A Model Mass Tort: The PPA Experience*, 54 DRAKE L. REV. 621, 638 (2006).
111. *See Wyeth v. Levine*, 555 U.S. 555, 571 (2009) (establishing the "clear evidence" standard).
112. *PLIVA, Inc. v. Mensing*, 564 U.S. 604, 623–24 (2011).
113. *In re Meridia*, 328 F. Supp. 2d at 813.
114. *In re Norplant Contraceptive Prods. Liab. Litig.*, 215 F. Supp. 2d 795, 828-829 (E.D. Tex. 2002).

115. *Id.* at 833.
116. *In re Temporomandibular Joint (TMJ) Implants Prods. Liab. Litig.*, 97 F.3d 1050, 1055 (8th Cir. 1996) (citation omitted).
117. United States Chamber Institute for Legal Reform, *MDL Proceedings: Eliminating the Chaff* 1 (2015).
118. *In re Heparin Prods. Liab. Litig.*, 803 F. Supp. 2d 712, 739 (N.D. Ohio 2011).
119. *In re Silica Prods. Liab. Litig.*, 398 F. Supp. 2d 563, 580 (S.D. Tex. 2002).
120. *Id.* at 632.
121. *Id.* at 635.
122. *Id.* at 636.
123. S. Todd Brown, *Plaintiff Control and Domination in Multidistrict Mass Torts*, 61 Clev. St. L. Rev. 391, 425 (2013).
124. *In re Digitek Prods. Liab. Litig.*, 821 F. Supp. 2d 822, 836 (S.D. W. Va. 2011).
125. *See* Washington Legal Foundation, *Multidistrict Litigation Reform: The Case for Earlier Application of Federal Pleading Standards*, No. 4, 1 (Sept. 2017).
126. *Ashcroft v. Iqbal*, 556 U.S. 662 (2009).
127. *Bell Atlantic Corp. v. Twombly*, 550 U.S. 544 (2007).
128. *In re Seroquel Prods. Liab. Litig.*, No. 6:06-md-1769, 2007 WL 737589, at *3 (M.D. Fla. Mar. 7, 2007).
129. Pre-Trial Order No. 65: Procedure for Severance of Multi-Plaintiff Cases, *In re: Taxotere (Docetaxel) Prods. Liab. Litig.*, No. 2:16-md-02740 (E.D. La. Oct. 16, 2017), E.C.F. No. 959.
130. *See* Ted Frank, *Welding Fume: A Disappearing Mass Tort?* Class Action Watch 9 (Mar. 2007).
131. *Id.* at 9.
132. *See* Case Administration Order, *In re Welding Fume Prods. Liab. Litig.*, No. 1:03-cv-17000 (N.D. Ohio Mar. 31, 2006), E.C.F. No. 1724.
133. *See* Ted Frank, *Welding Fume: A Disappearing Mass Tort?* Class Action Watch 9 (2007).
134. Bolch Judicial Institute, *Guidelines and Best Practices* at 13.
135. Eduardo C. Robreno, *The Federal Asbestos Product Liability Multidistrict Litigation (MDL-875): Black Hole or New Paradigm?* 23 Widener L.J. 97, 137–38 (2013).
136. *Id.* at 121.
137. *Id.*
138. *Amchem Prods., Inc. v. Windsor*, 521 U.S. 591, 631 (1997) (Breyer, J., concurring in part and dissenting in part) (citation omitted).
139. *In re Mentor Corp. Obtape Transobturator Sling*, 2016 WL 4705827, at *1.
140. *Id.*
141. *Id.*
142. Eldon Fallon et al., *Bellwether Trials in Multidistrict Litigation*, 82 Tulane L. Rev. 2323, 2333–34 (2008).
143. Washington Legal Foundation, *Multidistrict Litigation: Reducing Incentives for Abuse* 6 (Autumn 2017).
144. Lawyers for Civil Justice, *Request for Rulemaking* 4 (Aug. 10, 2017).
145. Federal Judicial Center, *Ten Steps* at 9–10.
146. 28 U.S.C. § 1407(a).
147. Bolch Judicial Institute, *Guidelines and Best Practices* at 1.

148. *Id.* at 104.
149. Federal Judicial Center, *Pocket Guide* at 45.
150. *Id.* at 45.
151. Eldon E. Fallon et al., *Bellwether Trials in Multidistrict Litigation*, 82 TUL. L. REV. 2323, 2343 (2008).
152. *Id.* at 2325.
153. *See, e.g.*, U.S. Chamber Institute for Legal Reform, *Trials and Tribulations: Contending with Bellwether and Multi-Plaintiff Trials in MDL Proceedings* (Oct. 2019).
154. *Id.* at 5.
155. *Lexecon Inc. v. Milberg Weiss Bershad Hynes & Lerach*, 523 U.S. 26 (1998).
156. *Id.* at 27.
157. Federal Judicial Center, *Ten Steps* at 9.
158. Bolch Judicial Institute, *Guidelines and Best Practices* at 22.
159. Federal Judicial Center, *Pocket Guide* at 44.
160. *See* Federal Judicial Center, *Ten Steps* at 8.
161. *See In re Motor Fuel Temperature Sales Practices Litig.*, 711 F.3d 1050, 1052 (9th Cir. 2013).
162. *See* Bolch Judicial Institute, *Guidelines and Best Practices* at 22.
163. Federal Judicial Center, *Pocket Guide* at 5.
164. U.S. Chamber Institute for Legal Reform, *Trials and Tribulations: Contending with Bellwether and Multi-Plaintiff Trials in MDL Proceedings* 7 (Oct. 2019).
165. Federal Judicial Center, *Manual for Complex Litigation*, Fourth § 22.315 (2004).
166. Eldon E. Fallon et al., *Bellwether Trials in Multidistrict Litigation*, 82 TUL. L. REV. 2323, 2362 (2008).
167. *Id.* at 2359 n.120.
168. Bolch Judicial Institute, *Guidelines and Best Practices* at 26.
169. *Id.*
170. *See id.* at 5.
171. Federal Judicial Center, *Pocket Guide* at 45–46.
172. *Id.* at 45.
173. Bolch Judicial Institute, *Guidelines and Best Practices* at 24.
174. *Id.* at 26–27.
175. Case Management Order No. 14C: Amendment to Trial Pool Selection, *In re: Taxotere (Docetaxel) Prods. Liab. Litig.*, No. 2:16-md-02740, at 3 (April 22, 2019).
176. *Id.*
177. Burch, *Mass Tort Deals* at 73–74.
178. *Graziose v. Am. Home Prods. Corp.*, 202 F.R.D. 638, 641 (D. Nev. 2001).
179. U.S. Chamber Institute for Legal Reform, *Trials and Tribulations: Contending with Bellwether and Multi-Plaintiff Trials in MDL Proceedings* 8 (Oct. 2019).
180. Bolch Judicial Institute, *Guidelines and Best Practices* at 25.
181. Federal Judicial Center, *Ten Steps* at 9.
182. Elizabeth Chamblee Burch, *Remanding Multidistrict Litigation*, 75 LA. L. REV. 399, 416 (2014).
183. Federal Judicial Center, *Pocket Guide* at 4.
184. David L. Noll, *MDL as Public Administration*, 118 MICH. L. REV. 403, 405 (2019).

185. *Id.*
186. Burch, *Mass Tort Deals* at 108.
187. *Id.*
188. *Id.* at 111–12.
189. *Id.* at 120.
190. Elizabeth Chamblee Burch, *Remanding Multidistrict Litigation*, 75 La. L. Rev. 399, 412 (2014).
191. Fed. R. Civ. P. 23(e).
192. *See, e.g.*, Burch, *Mass Tort Deals* at 111–12.
193. Federal Judicial Center, *Pocket Guide* at 41.
194. *Id.*
195. Bolch Judicial Institute, *Guidelines and Best Practices* at 108.
196. *Id.* at 109.
197. Federal Judicial Center, *Pocket Guide* at 41.
198. Bolch Judicial Institute, *Guidelines and Best Practices* at 101.
199. *See* Elizabeth Chamblee Burch, *Monopolies in Multidistrict Litigation*, 70 Vand. L. Rev. 67, 74–75 (2017).
200. *See* David L. Noll, *MDL as Public Administration*, 118 Mich. L. Rev. 403, 420 (2019).
201. *Id.*
202. Burch, *Mass Tort Deals* at 106.
203. *Id.*
204. *Id.*
205. Federal Judicial Center, *Pocket Guide* at 37.
206. *Amchem Prods., Inc. v. Windsor*, 521 U.S. 591 (1997).
207. *Ortiz v. Fibreboard Corp.*, 527 U.S. 815 (1999).
208. *Amchem*, 521 U.S. at 609, 624.
209. *Id.* at 626.
210. *Ortiz*, 527 U.S. at 853.
211. David L. Noll, *MDL as Public Administration*, 118 Mich. L. Rev. 403, 420–21 (2019).
212. *See* Jan Hoffman, *States Clash with Cities Over Potential Opioids Settlement Payouts*, N.Y. Times, Aug. 5, 2019; *In re: Nat'l Prescription Opiate Litig.*, No. 19-4097, –F.3d–, 2020 WL 5701916 (6th Cir. Sept. 24, 2020).
213. Advisory Committee on Civil Rules Minutes 201 (Oct. 29, 2019).
214. Federal Judicial Center, *Pocket Guide* at 27.
215. Douglas G. Smith, *The Myth of Settlement in MDL Proceedings*, 107 Ky. L.J. 467 (2018–2019).
216. Stephen J. Herman, *Duties Owed by Appointed Counsel to MDL Litigants Whom They Do Not Formally Represent*, 64 Loyola L. Rev. 1, 21 (2018).
217. *Id.*
218. *See* Burch, *Mass Tort Deals* at 74.
219. Eldon E. Fallon, *Common Benefit Fees in Multidistrict Litigation*, 74 La. L. Rev. 371, 379 (2014).
220. *See, e.g., JPML Sends Diet Drug Suits to Judge Bechtel in Eastern District of Pa.*, Andrews Mass Tort Litigation Reporter (Jan. 1998).
221. Federal Judicial Center, *Ten Steps* at 2.
222. Bolch Judicial Institute, *Guidelines and Best Practices* at 1, 2.

223. Elizabeth Chamblee Burch, *Judging Multidistrict Litigation*, 90 N.Y.U. L. REV. 71, 83–84 (2015).
224. Abbe R. Gluck, *Unorthodox Civil Procedure: Modern Multidistrict Litigation's Place in the Textbook Understandings of Procedure*, 165 U. PA. L. REV. 1669, 1673 (2017).
225. U.S. Chamber Institute for Legal Reform, *Trials and Tribulations: Contending with Bellwether and Multi-Plaintiff Trials in MDL Proceedings* 1 (Oct. 2019).
226. *See* David L. Noll, *MDL as Public Administration*, 118 MICH. L. REV. 403, 418–19 (2019).
227. *See* Federal Judicial Center, *Pocket Guide* at 24.
228. Bolch Judicial Institute, *Guidelines and Best Practices* at 81.
229. Abbe R. Gluck, *Unorthodox Civil Procedure: Modern Multidistrict Litigation's Place in the Textbook Understandings of Procedure*, 165 U. PA. L. REV. 1669, 1707 (2017).
230. Federal Judicial Center, *Pocket Guide* at 21–22.
231. *Id.* at 25.
232. Joint Coordination Order, *In re General Motors LLC Ignition Switch Litig.*, No. 1:14-md-02543 (S.D.N.Y. Sept. 24, 2014), ECF No. 315.
233. *Id.* at 3.
234. Federal Judicial Center, *Manual for Complex Litigation*, Fourth § 20.313 (2004).
235. Federal Judicial Center, *Ten Steps* at 6.
236. *Id.*
237. Bolch Judicial Institute, *Guidelines and Best Practices* at 34.
238. *Id.* at 90.
239. *Id.* at 91.
240. *See, e.g.*, Pre-Trial Order No. 15, *In re: Oil Spill by the Oil Rig "Deepwater Horizon" in the Gulf of Mexico, on April 20, 2010*, MDL 2179 (E.D. La., Nov. 5, 2010), E.C.F. No. 676; Order Regarding Remands, *In re: Nat'l Prescription Opiate Litig.*, No. 1:17-MD-2804 (N.D. Ohio Feb. 16, 2018), E.C.F. No. 130.
241. *See* Fed. R. Civ. P. 23(f).
242. *See* 28 U.S.C. § 1292(b).
243. Federal Judicial Center, *Ten Steps* at 6.
244. Federal Judicial Center, *Pocket Guide* at 25.
245. Abbe R. Gluck, *Unorthodox Civil Procedure: Modern Multidistrict Litigation's Place in the Textbook Understandings of Procedure*, 165 U. PA. L. REV. 1669, 1707 (2017).
246. *See In re Continental Airlines, Inc.*, 932 F.2d 282 (3d Cir. 1991).
247. *See, e.g., In re Nat'l Prescription Opiate Litig.*, No. 19-3935, 2019 WL 7482137 (6th Cir. Oct. 10, 2019); *In re Nat'l Prescription Opiate Litig.*, 783 Fed. Appx. 537 (6th Cir. Aug. 15, 2019).
248. *In re Nat'l Prescription Opiate Litig.*, 956 F.3d 838, 841 (6th Cir. 2020).
249. *Id.* at 842 (emphasis in original).
250. *Id.* at 843.
251. *Id.* (emphasis in original).
252. *Id.*
253. *Id.* at 841.
254. *Id.* at 844.

255. *Id.*
256. *Id.*
257. *In re Volkswagen of Am., Inc.*, 545 F.3d 304, 319 (5th Cir. 2008).
258. Burch, *Mass Tort Deals* at 150–51.
259. *See* Ed Crooks, *More than 100 Jailed for Fake BP Oil Spill Claims*, FINANCIAL TIMES, Jan. 15, 2017.
260. *See* Mark A. Behrens & William F. Northrip, *Department of Justice Combats Asbestos Trust Abuse*, 86 DEFENSE COUNSEL J. 1 (Jan. 2019).
261. *See, e.g.*, Lawyers for Civil Justice, *MDL Practices and the Need for FRCP Amendments: Proposals for Discussion with the MDL/TPLF Subcommittee of the Advisory Committee on Civil Rules* (Sept. 14, 2018), https://www.uscourts.gov/sites/default/files/suggestion_18-cv-x_0.pdf.
262. Draft Minutes Civil Rules Advisory Committee 17 (April 2–3, 2019).
263. *Id.*
264. Fairness in Class Action Litigation Act of 2017, H.R. 985, 115th Cong. (2017).
265. *Id.*
266. Minutes of the Committee on Rules of Practice and Procedure 17 (June 25, 2019).
267. Fairness in Class Action Litigation Act of 2017, H.R. 985, 115th Cong. § 105(i) (2017).
268. Fairness in Class Action Litigation Act of 2017, H.R. 985, 115th Cong. (2017).
269. Draft Minutes Civil Rules Advisory Committee 21 (April 2–3, 2019).
270. Advisory Committee on Civil Rules Minutes 195 (Oct. 29, 2019).
271. Minutes of the Advisory Committee on Civil Rules 204 (Oct. 29, 2019).
272. *See, e.g.*, Brian Devine, *Interlocutory Appeals in MDLs Would Burden Litigants, Courts*, LAW360 (Apr. 24, 2020).
273. *See* Draft Minutes Civil Rules Advisory Committee 21 (April 2–3, 2019).
274. *See* David L. Noll, *MDL as Public Administration*, 118 MICH. L. REV. 403, 464 (2019).
275. Fairness in Class Action Litigation Act of 2017, H.R. 985, 115th Cong. (2017).
276. *Lexecon*, 523 U.S. at 27.
277. Federal Judicial Center, *Pocket Guide* at 5.
278. Draft Minutes Civil Rules Advisory Committee 17 (April 2–3, 2019).
279. Minutes of the Advisory Committee on Civil Rules 206 (Oct. 29, 2019).
280. *Id.* at 214.
281. *Id.*
282. *See* John Rabiej, *Two Proposals to Improve How Courts Manage "Mega-MDLs,"* available at https://www.law.gwu.edu/sites/g/files/zaxdzs2351/f/downloads/rabiej.mdlpaper.pdf.
283. *See* Initial Case Management Scheduling Order re General Causation at 1–2, *In re: Incretin Mimetics Prods. Liab. Litig.*, No. 13-MD-2452 (S.D. Cal. Feb. 18, 2014), ECF No. 325.
284. 28 U.S.C. § 1407.
285. *In re Depuy Orthopaedics, Inc.*, 870 F.3d 345, 351 (5th Cir. 2017).
286. Bolch Judicial Institute, *Guidelines and Best Practices* at vii (analyzing data from the Administrative Office of the United States Courts).
287. Edward F. Sherman, *When Remand Is Appropriate in Multidistrict Litigation*, 75 LA. L. REV. 455, 456 (2014).

288. Bolch Judicial Institute, *Guidelines and Best Practices* at 93.
289. *Id.* at 94.
290. Elizabeth Chamblee Burch, *Remanding Multidistrict Litigation*, 75 La. L. Rev. 399, 404 (2014).
291. Federal Judicial Center, *Pocket Guide* at 48.
292. *Id.*
293. Burch, *Mass Tort Deals* at 208.
294. Bolch Judicial Institute, *Guidelines and Best Practices* at 105.
295. *See, e.g.*, Brendan Pierson, *U.S. Judge Rules Talc Lawsuits Against J&J Can Proceed, Testimony Limited*, Reuters, Apr. 27, 2020.
296. Fed. R. Civ. P. 23.
297. Fed. R. Civ. P. 23(b)(3).
298. *Amchem Prods., Inc. v. Windsor*, 521 U.S. 591 (1997).
299. *Ortiz v. Fibreboard Corp.*, 527 U.S. 815 (1999).
300. Edward F. Sherman, *When Remand is Appropriate in Multidistrict Litigation*, 75 La. L. Rev. 455, 467 (2014).
301. Federal Judicial Center, *Pocket Guide* at 37.
302. *In re Zyprexa Prods. Liab. Litig.*, 238 F.R.D. 539, 542 (E.D.N.Y. 2006).
303. Brian T. Fitzpatrick, *The Conservative Case for Class Actions* (2019).
304. *See* Edith H. Jones, *Rough Justice in Mass Future Claims: Should Bankruptcy Courts Direct Tort Reform?* 76 Tex. L. Rev. 1695 (1998).
305. *See* Douglas G. Smith, *Resolution of Mass Tort Claims in the Bankruptcy System*, 41 U.C. Davis L. Rev. 1613 (2008).
306. *In re Walker*, 51 F.3d 562, 566 (5th Cir. 1995).
307. *See* Douglas G. Smith, *Resolution of Mass Tort Claims in the Bankruptcy System*, 41 U.C. Davis L. Rev. 1631 (2008).
308. 28 U.S.C. § 1334(b).
309. Georgene Vairo, *Mass Tort Bankruptcies: The Who, The Why and The How*, 78 Bankr. L.J. 93, 125 (2003).
310. *See* 11 U.S.C. § 524(g)(1)(A).
311. *See In re Dow Corning Corp.*, 215 B.R. 346 (Bankr. E.D. Mich. 1997).
312. *See In re Dow Corning Corp.*, 86 F.3d 482, 493 (6th Cir. 1996) (discussing the *Robins* ruling).
313. *In re A.H. Robins, Inc.*, 862 F.2d 1092, 1093 (4th Cir. 1988).
314. Georgene M. Vairo, *The Dalkon Shield Claimants Trust: Paradigm Lost (or Found)?* 61 Fordham L. Rev. 617, 655–56 (1992).
315. *See id.*
316. Tina Bellon and Tom Hals, *Johnson & Johnson Supplier Seeks Bankruptcy Over Talc Lawsuits*, Reuters, Feb. 13, 2019.
317. Vanessa Romo, *Insys Files for Chapter 11, Days After Landmark Opioid Settlement of $225 Million*, NPR, June 10, 2019.
318. Mike Spector, *OxyContin Maker Purdue Pharma Files for Bankruptcy Protection*, Reuters, Sept. 15, 2019.

About the Author

Douglas Smith is a lawyer who practices in Chicago, Illinois. For more than two decades, he worked at Kirkland & Ellis LLP where he was a partner. Before that, he was a law clerk to the Honorable David Sentelle of the U.S. Court of Appeals for the D.C. Circuit. He has taught various courses at the Antonin Scalia Law School at George Mason University School of Law and Loyola University Chicago School of Law. He obtained his law degree from the Northwestern Pritzker School of Law, an M.B.A. from The University of Chicago Booth School of Business, and a B.S. and B.A. from the State University of New York at Buffalo. He is a member of the American Law Institute and has published more than 40 scholarly articles on a variety of legal topics.

Index

P

R

S

V

W